Unlimited Property Investing Success Using E

Buy, Refurbish, Refinanc

(Bonus Chapter on the Final 'R' for Retire!)

Peter J How

Disclaimer

Although the author and publisher have made every effort to ensure that the information in this book was correct at the time of publication, the author and publisher do not assume and hereby disclaim any liability to any party for any loss, damage, or disruption, caused by errors or omissions, whether such errors or omissions result from negligence, accident, or any other cause.

You are strongly advised to take professional advice from a qualified financial advisor before making any decisions of a financial nature. This will allow for the specifics of your situation to be understood and proposed actions either supported or modified. The same applies to any decisions regarding taxation and pensions for the same reasons, you are strongly advised to discuss your ideas and proposals with a qualified advisor before taking action. Again, this will allow for the specifics of your situation to be understood and proposed actions either supported or modified.

Copyright

Dedication

To those who wish to make a change in their lives through property investment,

but never thought they had the money to do it with.

I was once in your shoes, and here I share with you my main learnings along the way.

Get ready for an exciting yet challenging ride.

Leave your stamp behind in this world,

with all the property deals and property changes you make.

All of which is part and parcel of the BRRRR property investing strategy.

About the Property Investing Series

The Property Investing Series offers concise information-packed guides for learning and future easy-reference and provides information on further resources for additional information.

The content of the books is based on the author's personal experience and knowledge of property investing mostly in England, together with contributions from other Property Experts' knowledge where appropriate. Very similar practices to those in England are also used in the rest of the UK, although there are sometimes slight variations in each particular country due to legislation, of which you will become aware, but the principles are the same.

When the author first started investing in property, there was not as much information available as there is today in the form of books, publications and property courses. Most of the information back then was from America, and he used this to work out how to successfully invest in property in the UK. He was, therefore, more aware of the American financial and real-estate system than that of his own country and had to make the necessary adaptations for the differences.

This third book, in what will be a series of guides, can also serve as a model for general understanding by anyone, from any country, provided they then find out how such ideas relate to their particular country where they are investing in property. Usually, most of the principles are often the same, although there can be a few notable differences you will quickly become aware of.

The first book, called *All About Buy-to-Let Mortgages*, covered in detail how to fully finance your property empire. This is a very important part of the topic of this present book and some of the principles are represented here. The second book, *UK Property Investment: The Toxic Truth!* focusses more on the practicalities of lettings, which are the most challenging aspect of the BRRRR investing strategy known to many simply as BRR, which is now fully covered in detail in this present book.

The contents page, chapters and headings in the books are structured for highlighting the key topics within each subject area. This should therefore give a framework for easy understanding and quick review, as well as helping with future reference.

For those wanting additional information, in each book, there are references to further resources and, where appropriate, the opportunity to obtain property investor *insider knowledge*. Such knowledge is usually only made available at the often very expensive property training courses and academies.

How to Contact the Author

For anyone needing to contact me, the author, about this book then please use the email address contact@peterjhow.com

Due to my busy schedule, please allow 24 hours during the working week for a response to your email, although I will endeavour to answer quicker than this if at all possible.

The email address of contact@peterjhow.com is also the one to use for all media enquiries including TV, radio, and print.

If you would like to obtain copies of this book in print and bulk at a discount, perhaps to give away to your clients, colleagues or employees, then please indicate the number of copies that you think you will require and I will make an appropriate proposal to you.

I am also happy to receive any constructive comments and suggestions for future editions of the book, where this will make the information presented even better.

Of course, the amount of information included has to be carefully controlled to make sure that the subject matter is easily understandable, and not something that will confuse people. Please don't be disappointed if you make some positive suggestions, then later I decide that these are not suitable for inclusion in future editions of the book. I can assure you that I value all feedback and treat any improvement suggestions very seriously.

For those readers who are also property experts in their particular field, and would like to discuss a co-publishing deal with me, please send an outline of your expertise for consideration at the email address given.

If this book stimulates your further interest in investing in UK property, you should learn how to get the best financing available for your property investment programme.

Being able to understand how to best use mortgages and remortgages is a cornerstone of the BRRRR approach to investing.

Download your FREE book summary of my first book
All About Buy-to-Let Mortgages:

www.buy-to-let-mortgages.org.uk/bonus

To find out more about the additional

information, products and services go to:

www.buy-to-let-mortgages.org.uk

Table of Contents

Preface

The first property investing book I wrote was *All About Buy-to-Let Mortgages*, which was published in June 2017 and released on Amazon. I did nothing else to market it because I wanted to get my book companion website completed before I did that. Well, the website development took on a story of its own and took a lot longer to complete than I thought it would.

During that time, the book was steadily selling on Amazon in gradually increasing numbers without any marketing effort on my part. The reviews, although few, were very good. I would, therefore, like to take this early opportunity to ask you to give this book a review when you have read it, as it seems very hard to get reviews without specifically asking.

Please, therefore, hold it in mind to make the effort to give me a review at the end of this book. It really will encourage me to write more books, as I will get more exposure as an author if you give me a review.

Anyway, I wrote my first book as an investor who had learnt from many years of experience as to how to get the best out of mortgage finance, as well as getting the best from mortgage brokers. That book contains ways of creatively financing deals that you may already broadly understand in principle, but not in the detail that the book goes into on clarifying exactly HOW to do it.

In my second book, *UK Property Investment: The Toxic Truth!* , I spilt the beans on what it is likely to mean to your life to be a property investor, and particularly one investing in UK buy-to-let property. That book is focussed on the more difficult-to-handle side to property investment that is very seldom mentioned elsewhere.

If you need to know more about the positives after learning about the negatives (whether by reading my book or from experience with investing), look out for the future sequel that I fully expect to write and will be aptly called ***UK Property Investment: The Antidote!***

I think that is an appropriate title for the sequel to 'The Toxic Truth' as there are positives that are needed to enable you to shoulder the negatives I mention in the book. Whether the 'antidote' will be sufficient for the future is another matter, only time will tell as all UK Government's seem hell-bent on making the UK property investment business as difficult as possible in recent years.

In this book, I reveal the main component parts of what is commonly known as the BRRRR investing strategy. This stands for Buy, Refurbish, Refinance, Rent, Repeat. When I first started out with this it was simply termed BRR (the other two terms were omitted). However, as with all things, changes are made and now we have the other terms added which are Rent and Repeat. These two additional 'R' actions were always implied in BRR of course, but now they are often talked about in the same sentence. Although it is still commonly referred to by many as simply BRR; it is the same thing.

To explain the order of Refinance and Rent in the acronym, I have chosen to keep it as it originally was in BRR with the third 'R' being for Refinance. However, with a fairly recent change in the allowable time before a Refinance can be easily put in place to be six months, it may be the case that you Rent out before refinancing. This will depend on the extent of the refurbishment programme. Insurance companies will also be looking for you to rent the property out soon after purchase, unless you have special property refurbishment insurance in place.

To add my own stamp on things, I want to take the BRRRR one step further and call it the BRRRR(R!) method, because the extra 'R' stands for Retire. That, for most people, will be their ultimate objective and motivation in being interested in this investing strategy in the first place. It therefore should take the pride of place at the end of the line-up of letters in the sequence. I have therefore included a bonus chapter on retiring and in particular on retiring from your activities with property investing using the BRRRR approach. Maybe the exclamation mark can be seen an expression of relief, after dealing with all that I am about to tell you about BRRRR.

In this book, I will reveal the many lessons that have led me all the way to the final additional R of retirement. However, what you might define as retirement may differ between people. Some would say I am still so active that there is no way I can consider myself retired. However, I managed to quit the well-paid day job and do what I want to do now, which is my definition of retirement. Consider what your definition is and make sure what you do is leading you towards that goal.

I have tried to pack into this book all the main things that I have learned over the past 16 years of investing in UK property, as far as it relates to BRRRR. If you are just starting out with property investment, this book will act as a great guide to prepare you for the journey and tackle all of what awaits you. You can then take advantage of all the opportunities and reduce the impact of any potential negative matters. To be forewarned is to be forearmed, as the saying goes.

If you have already started and are currently active in property investment, I am sure you will still be able to benefit from what I teach here, if only to fill in some gaps in your knowledge that you have gained so far. I always seem to learn something from any book I read, no matter how well acquainted I am with the subject matter under discussion.

Note that this book is about *Residential* Property Investment and not Commercial Property, which is much different. However, most property investors prefer residential property so this will appeal to a wider audience. Similar principles would however apply to commercial property and you can get the same benefits of taking the BRRRR approach, should you choose to go down that alternative property investment path.

Finally, I would like to make a point concerning the predominant property type that I have invested in, which are the lower cost and higher-yielding type properties. These properties are *exactly* the kind of investment properties that many property courses encourage you to buy as an investor.

Fasten your seatbelt for an exhilarating ride on your property investing journey. I sincerely hope you make it to the Retirement step sooner than you expect.

14

Introduction

This book is for those who want to

- Learn from someone with 16 years of experience in property investment.
- Understand how BRRRR works and how to plan to add an additional 'R' for Retire!
- Be prepared to take the plunge as a property investor, even if you have little money.
- Be informed about the details of BRRRR property investing and how to get the most from it.

It is also suitable for those who just want to know what BRRRR really is and how it is used by property investors in the UK, investing in buy-to-let properties.

I write this as someone who needed mortgage finance in order to invest in property. In fact, I had only £5,000 in the bank, which was not enough to start out in buy-to-let (BTL). However, by using mortgage money, I have been able to go on to buy over 40 properties in the last 16 years. This would have been more apart from the world financial crisis we had when mortgage lending availability, as a result, was reduced drastically for a period immediately afterwards.

All the money in these properties is mortgaged money, so I have learnt to use the UK mortgage finance system in quite an advanced way to achieve this. My book *All About Buy-to-Let Mortgages* covers how I achieved this and what I learnt along the way.

Now, in this book, I focus on the additional matters concerning the BRRRR approach to Property Investment, using very little of your own money. Note, that for brevity in this Audible version of the book, I will shorten BRRRR to simply BRR, which is the term by which it is also commonly known, unless otherwise demanded by context. If you are new to property investing, by carefully studying this book, you will soon be way ahead of those who are just going to learn by experience. In doing so, you will be much better prepared for what is awaiting you rather than just learning by experience, like I had to do.

Studying the contents of this book and gaining a good understanding of the challenges involved in buy-to-let property investment will pay off financially for you in the end. Just *learning by doing* in anything almost always turns out to be expensive. For sure, we learn from our mistakes, however, it is much better to learn from the knowledge of others who have gone before us and made mistakes and discoveries which they can share for our benefit.

It is also true to say that things have not stayed the same over the 16 years I have been investing in property, I have to say regrettably. However, in the property investment business, you have to keep adapting to the changes and keep in touch with the changes taking place. You can then adjust and adapt to the property investing climate at any particular time.

In the UK, we currently have many rules and regulations that give us certain challenges which other countries may not have to face, where we are disadvantaged compared to property investors in those other countries. However, we also have some facilities in buy-to-let finance which are not available in most other countries, and this is mostly to our advantage compared to other countries (I have covered all of this in my book *All About Buy-to-Let Mortgages*).

This book will equip you with the knowledge to work, either by yourself or with an investment partner, on getting the best property investment approach that suits your personality and personal situation. This could easily save you a lot of heartache and pain compared to learning by experience alone, especially as it relates to carefully managing your investment money (whether it is yours or Other People's Money).

Be aware, there are many books readily available on property investment that only emphasise the positives of being involved in the BRRRR process. This could be misleading if you are only expecting good things to happen.

There is, maybe unsurprisingly, very little information available about the challenges that BRRRR property investors face. Of the information that can be found, often in the form of comments on social media, I have found these to be very selective in what they say and there are many gaps in the information.

I can understand that maybe those offering property training courses need to be careful about what they tell you. After all, they are in the market of selling the property courses that make them money, rather than selflessly preparing you for what you are considering entering into. However, if any such courses refer you to this book before you 'jump in', or if they share with you much of the information contained in this book, they will be giving you a very good service.

The absolute worst time to learn about it is when you have committed to it and cannot change direction easily, without possibly incurring significant lost amounts of money as you exit. It could cost you dearly to change your mind and move out of property investment when you run into some of the issues I highlight in this book.

This book will prepare you to get into BRRRR property investment in the best frame of mind. Go ahead and set out your stall to study and profit from the information contained in this book. When you face the issues I mention, you will be well-prepared to tackle them head-on, and you will be glad you took the time to equip yourself for your journey ahead.

About the Author

I have worked in the manufacturing industry as an employee pretty much since leaving school. I say *pretty much* because my first year was spent on property… on the lowest rung of the ladder… cleaning windows (no pun intended!). That was my first business venture, where my friend and I would wake up around midday and then go to clean some windows. We did this for some extra cash after leaving school at 16 and watching our old school friends and our girlfriends (one each of course!) go to sixth form college.

I just wanted to start work. However, it was 1980 and it was at the beginning of a recession, therefore it was not the best time for someone to find a job. Especially having left school with only a solitary GCSE 'O' Level in English! Nevertheless, after about one year of trying to find a job by walking around the local industries, I managed to get set on as an apprentice electrician. I chose this as my work preference simply because an older cousin of mine was an electrician and it seemed quite technical and therefore interesting to me.

Anyway, we sold the window cleaning business for a few quid to some other aspiring souls and left for our full-time jobs. My friend got a job down a coal mine. Yes, this was before the Thatcher years, and yes, I was born and brought up in the North of England. Apart from inside the pub occasionally, I never really saw much of my friend after that because he worked a very complicated shift pattern down the mine.

But in the end, I wanted to be more than an electrician and went to the local college to study on day-release and night classes, doing engineering studies beyond what was required for me to complete my apprenticeship. This then led to me climbing back up the academic ladder, going away to University as a full-time student and even getting a First Class Honours Bachelor of Engineering Degree.

It was hard work. Although it just shows what you can do when you are interested in something and want to rise to a challenge. I took great pleasure in blowing away all those ex-sixth-formers at University as none of them got a First! It was just two others and I who got first-class honours degrees out of our studies. Interestingly, these other two people had also come the same route as me, by part-time study to get into University (OK, Polytechnic as it was then, but University as it is called now, and University sounds better anyway!).

Not to be defeated by thinking I could only get a top result at Polytechnic, I later enrolled on a Master's Degree course run by the University and came out on top again with a *Pass with Distinction*. I was the only one to get that I recall. I was then asked by the University if I would do a doctorate. However, that was to be the end of my academic studies for me as far as my appetite went (I mean... to go from Window Cleaner to Doctor?!). By then I had simply had enough studying and just wanted to go and do some work and try to make a difference in the big wide world!

Out in the professional working world, I did quite well by climbing up the corporate ladder and having, at one point, a Factory full of people I was responsible for as a Factory Manager. During the early years of my career, I had spent some time doing technical training, this was on the use and maintenance of bespoke manufacturing equipment. It meant I had to write technical manuals as well as run the courses for the engineers and manufacturing staff. This led to me taking a course in Technical Authorship, where I gained a recognised qualification for this through the City & Guilds of London Institute.

I hope you will find that my training and experience in technical authorship helps me communicate some of the more involved content clearly and understandably. However, as is often quoted, "Everything should be made as simple as possible, but no simpler."

Anyway, after climbing up the corporate ladder I came unstuck with some organisational politics, conflicting with some people in high places. I slid down a snake, or that is how it felt if you can imagine a career as a game of snakes and ladders! However, I was offered an alternative employment position where I could be very creative and enjoy what I do, rather than be drawn into company political matters.

The new job role was much more sheltered from the politics that I hated. I hated the fact that you had to support those above you, irrespective of whether you thought they were right or wrong. The problem for me was that I would simply not do that, so I guess I paid the price for it. That is fair enough - if that is how the senior corporate world works. It's not for me.

At some point about 16 years ago, I started to show an interest in the property market in the UK. In fact, I did look at this even before then, about 20 years ago. That would have been a much better time to have started in property investment. Property prices increased so much in those five years and even doubled in value in the area I was living. Anyway, we can only benefit from the time we decide to start in property and that determines our story.

Mine has been a story of learning by doing and then benefiting from property price increases, before suffering from the sudden drop in prices due to the financial crisis in 2008. Then seeing some benefit in low-interest rates, helping me to get the cash to support the properties, rather than relying on making money when I sold, which was my original intention.

As I said, I learnt by doing to start with, making lots of costly mistakes. Then I decided to attend some of those apparently expensive property courses. Well, they seemed expensive but quite cheap compared to the money I had lost from simply learning from experience. However, by the time I attended the courses I had learnt first-hand most of what they were teaching. Although you can always learn more and I am sure I got my money back and more, just from a few tips I picked up on the courses and applied to my investing.

Now, after 16 years of part-time property investment, whilst also keeping up a full-time day job, I have decided to write down what I have learnt in a series of books that I am calling The Property Investing Series. I continued to work simply because I quite enjoyed my day job, it was quite well paid and had a company car and other benefits... so quite hard to give up if you don't have to. However, with the advent of some of the changes that came to taxation, I chose to retire from my job as the recently introduced property taxation obligations involved in working full-time and having property held in my own name became too onerous.

I now continue just with property and plan to make my property investing series writing an up-to-date venture, by providing further information that will be accessible from the internet. Additionally, making the reader interaction available on the internet for the specific subjects covered, where appropriate. This is therefore much more than just a book-writing venture, it's intended to be a property investment resource provision venture that should give you more benefits than if I simply just wrote and published books alone.

You might be wondering where I am, at the time of writing, in my property investment world? Well, I have over 40 properties and each one is fully financed by bank or mortgage lender finance. This is often referred to as owning property with No Money Down (or No Money Left In, to be more precise). I achieved this using the same BRRRR approach that I describe in detail in this book.

I have experience in a wide range of tenant sectors as well as different property types (large and small terraced houses, semi-detached, leasehold flats, and detached houses with large gardens). Also, I have experience in various tenanting models, from single-family lets to houses in multiple occupation. And latterly serviced accommodation, which is quickly growing in popularity.

The estimated total value of my property portfolio is currently just over the **three and a half million pounds** mark, and I now have people who work with me full-time and part-time to keep the properties ticking over with new tenants. This is for tenanting the multi-let houses in which rooms in houses are let on an individual room tenancy basis, and preparing and managing single lets and serviced accommodation. I then have other people who maintain the properties for me on a daily hands-on basis.

As stated, I recently retired from my day job and leave the day-to-day management of my properties to my property management company. I am still fairly actively involved in the running of my property portfolio and regularly attend courses in the property investment sector. However, I currently do this over the phone and by internet connection, as I mostly live abroad now with my partner in Costa Rica.

My author name, as you can see from the cover, is **PETER J HOW**. I wanted my name to mean something to you, something that will help you with your property investment journey. Therefore, think of my name this way… **P**roperty **E**xpert **T**eaching **E**veryone **R**esponsibly **J**ust **HOW** to invest in property.

You can work out my age from some facts mentioned earlier, this will test your basic maths ability; which you will need for property investing, but nothing any more complicated, fortunately.

I make that my aim to teach you to invest **Responsibly** by making you aware of both the upsides and the possible downsides to the property ventures you can get involved in.

I could have been much younger writing this if I had started in property investment at a more tender age. However, I like to think of our age-in-property because we can all start at different times in our life. What matters is our unique property journey and how we benchmark where we are in terms of how long we have been investing to see how well we are doing.

Even then, this is affected by our unique character, which in turn can determine such things as your level of risk-taking which can impact on how quickly your portfolio grows. The main thing is to get into the property investment game and stay in there. Don't make big mistakes like some have done and then gone bankrupt. Not many go bankrupt, but some do. You have been warned. Treat the approaches described in this book with respect, and take professionally qualified financial advice when applying anything to your personal situation.

Buy

Your First Property

Taking the plunge and making your first property purchase can be quite daunting. I remember very well my first property purchase. I had read all the books I needed to be able to educate myself to a level to give me the confidence to go ahead, but it was still a heart-stopping moment when the offer I made on a property was accepted. There was every reason for it to be that way because that was a pivotal moment that changed my life ahead forever.

I was not sure why I was so nervous. It could have been the sheer amount of money I was dealing with or the fact that, due to lack of experience, I was buying into something I was not fully sure about. At least not fully comfortable with in terms of experience and therefore my confidence was low. In my head, my confidence was high, because I had learned about the topic in quite some detail. Yet in my heart, there were doubts due to the lack of experience I just mentioned. At least that is how I remember it all now, but it seems a very long time ago.

I mention this because it will very likely be a similar experience for you if you are just considering starting or making your first tentative steps into the world of property. You will probably have read property investment books or completed one of the many training courses (which can vary massively in terms of educational quality). However, depending on your temperament, maybe nothing can quite prepare you for that first step, you can only prepare yourself.

Of course, how you feel at your first property purchase will depend on your personality, and largely on your attitude to risk. This is where there are often differences of opinion about purchasing property, in particular investment property. Most of us will be well accustomed to the idea of buying a property for residential purposes, by taking out a very large loan that will likely take nearly a working lifetime to pay off. But to do this many times and accumulate a portfolio of investment properties is quite a different thing.

If you talk to the average person in the street about this, it is most likely you will be looked at by them in a way that asks the question as to whether you are crazy. This is because the mindset required to serially buy investment property and build a business out of it is something that most people will even not have considered. This is unless of course, they had the cash sat in the bank. Not many people are fortunate enough to have such large bank accounts but if you did have so much money, you would be stupid to keep it in the bank in this low-interest rate environment.

Therefore, other than already being a multi-millionaire, investment in property, especially for those with very little money in their bank accounts, is often seen as a very risky venture. If you are not well-prepared, that is something which could turn out very much to be the case. I know of investors that started at the same time as me and quickly ended up going bankrupt after only a few years. When I speak to them about it, they say it seemed like it was a quick win to make easy money, but then it quickly turned into a liability when they could not generate the money to pay the mortgages they had taken out. Repossession then shortly followed, resulting in bankruptcy due to a negative equity situation, as the properties were worth much less than they had paid for them.

Because of this risk, it is right to be very careful about making your first investment and getting off to a good start. As you make your first investment and see it largely go to plan, this will be a confidence booster for you. It will help springboard you onto other investments and help you start to grow your portfolio of properties. However, many people falter at this first step, yet this very step holds the keys to the plans which you have in mind.

I don't have the exact statistics, and I am not sure that anyone will have the true figures, but the percentage of people who consider property investment and build a sizeable portfolio of properties is very small. Of those who attend one of the many training courses, I have heard several times from different sources, that the percentage of people who progress to buying investment properties is in the single figure range.

I am pretty sure that if the people not taking action would have only made their first purchase, it would have been a very different story for them. If you have already bought your first investment property, I think you will relate to what I am saying. If you have not taken this step yet then I hope my honesty about this matter will help you to do so.

Perhaps the best mindset to have about this is to think about what is the absolute worst that can happen. You might have heard this said before, but it is a good way to look at things. If you can stomach what you consider is the worst thing that can happen, then go ahead and plan to avoid whatever that thing is as best you can.

Your first investment property purchase should also be treated as a learning experience. This is when you draw on all the knowledge you have gained and start to put it into practice. However, there is often a large difference between theory and practice in any subject, and property investment is no different. Your lessons from experience will fill the gaps in your property knowledge very quickly.

I would say that by the time you are onto your fifth property purchase, you will have gained the confidence you need to see you through a lifetime of investing. But to get there you need to make that first purchase. I am reminded of that well-known Chinese proverb that states a journey of a thousand miles starts with a single step. These are very wise words, particularly when it comes to starting out in property investing.

Therefore, go out there and make your first investment property purchase, if you still need to do that. It is the springboard to what you are taking the time to read about here. None of the information in this book will be of any use to you without taking that very first vital step.

Profitability Calculations

After all that I have just said, regarding taking the plunge to buy your first property, you need to carefully consider many of the following matters raised in this chapter. Not least of which are the profitability calculations. When you have managed to secure a property purchase, you want it to be an asset to you and not a liability. That is to say, you want to have it put money in your pocket rather than take it away from you.

This is unlike our domestic homes, where we are accustomed to paying bills from other income sources. That makes our homes liabilities in reality, despite the hope of capital appreciation that they bring us, which we often look at as pure profit. I mean, how many of your own domestic homes do you think you could support? Making money from our investment properties is therefore necessary, even if we were investing in the hope of eventual long-term significant capital appreciation. Now with this in mind, let us take a look at some of the key metrics for property profitability assessment.

The *Gross Yield* on a buy-to-let property is the expected or actual annual rental income expressed as a percentage of purchase price or property valuation. Often the word *Gross* is dropped and just the term *Yield* is used to describe gross yield, that is something to be aware of in the use of property investment jargon.

For single-let houses, the gross yield is typically somewhere in the range of a few percent in locations where the price of property is very high compared to the cost of renting (such as in London), to a maximum of low double-digit percentages in areas of lower-cost properties (such as in the North of England).

The gross yield is a good figure to use in order to assess whether your income from the rental of the property is likely to cover your mortgage payments. It certainly should be higher than the interest rate that you are going to have to pay on the mortgage. The higher the gross yield the better, to give you income sufficient enough to cover empty periods and inevitable maintenance costs.

Often it is best to do a quick calculation of gross yield to see if it is in a region of giving a return you will be happy with, to comfortably support the costs associated with ownership. If this calculation comes out OK, you can then do a more detailed analysis. This deeper analysis would add up all the costs over a year and even allow for the costs of the property being empty and bad debt estimation (typically rental defaults and associated costs). You then subtract these from the income potential over the year to leave you with the net income.

Recently, in property investment circles, more focus has been put on what is termed *Net Yield* to ensure that this is positive. If this is positive then it should give positive cash flow, ensuring the properties can be held securely for a long period to allow time for capital appreciation, which has been much slower to non-existent in some areas in recent years.

Net yield is what is left after all the costs have been paid; this is including the finance costs of mortgage interest payments and property maintenance and servicing costs. It should include any cost that can be attributed to having ownership of the property. It can then be expressed as a percentage of the property price or valuation figure to give it in percentage terms. To be more meaningful, net yield can be usefully left expressed in terms of profit (or loss) per month or per annum, rather than a percentage.

In this calculation, you want to be left with a positive figure which is the net profit expected to be made after all costs have been deducted. If this is negative, it means you have to put money towards owning the property, in addition to contributing all the rental income to it. In this way, it is costing money from your pocket just to own the property. The more negative the figure the more it will cost you.

There is currently a prevailing focus on higher-yielding investment strategies with buy-to-let that provides a considerable net yield. However, these then often require more work in maintaining the running of the property portfolio. Typically, this involves a higher turnover of tenants when renting out rooms (houses in multiple occupation) or running serviced accommodation for the short term (typically having guests for just a few days to a few weeks at a time).

It can also include maximising housing benefit income if you are renting to tenants in that sector. This would involve ensuring you get a mix of housing benefit claiming tenants that can represent two households living in the same dwelling, on a joint tenancy agreement.

In this way, you can legally and rightfully get paid the benefit that each party is entitled to, based on their assessed need for housing. This also means that even if they make do with fewer bedrooms than entitled to, they can still claim for their full entitlement.

However, this all then becomes less of a so-called passive income and more of an actively earned income, unless you can afford to pay someone else to take on this increased property management activity. Interestingly, many property investment teachers and courses, still frequently refer to such property investment income as passive income. The reality is that these higher-yielding properties generally require a high level of work input to make them work.

Refinancing Calculations

The term *refinancing* usually simply means remortgaging in the UK. In the UK, we are more used to word *mortgage* as a loan secured against a property, therefore a refinance is the same thing as a remortgage. This is just terminology as *refinancing* is a more widely-used international term to describe the same thing, as far as property is concerned. For sake of focus on UK property matters, we will therefore be using the more common term of *remortgage* rather than *refinance*, but both in the context of this book mean the same thing.

Generally, you can remortgage a property after six months of ownership, although there are exceptions where this can be done sooner. Because you already own the property, your deposit money and any additional equity are already invested in it. Therefore, on remortgaging, you should only need to pay more money to cover the completion costs of solicitor's fees, valuation fees, and the lender's charges.

After six months of ownership, the true market value of the property should be taken as the property value for lending purposes, irrespective of what you bought it for. If you bought it at a bargain price and also added some value to the property by putting in a small amount to refurbish it, such as a new kitchen and bathroom for example, and general decoration upgrade, you could be owning a property that can be remortgaged at a much higher value than the price you paid for it. This is a summary of the process involved in first two terms of Buy and Refurbish in the BRRRR process.

If you were to take just a 75% LTV mortgage against this new higher valuation, the money paid to you on remortgage could be as high as the total amount of money you have put into the deal in the first place. (You may also be able to get 80% or even 85% mortgages, depending on the prevailing lending appetite, which makes it easier to do.) In this case, you will get paid back an amount of money by the solicitor to an account of your choice, which is the balance left after you draw down the remortgage amount. This is how you effectively create a 100% BRRRR financing situation or leaving No Money Left In.

Additional property value created from improvement work is sometimes called *sweat equity*, although in most cases you don't have to do much sweating as you don't need to do the work to improve the property yourself. Instead, you can get some reliable tradesmen to do this work for you. This is nearly always a better option considering the cost of your time versus their expertise and efficiency. Other more formal terms used to describe this increase in value activity is simply *Adding Value* or *Forced Appreciation*, as we will discuss later.

Let's illustrate this 100% cash-out remortgage example with some example figures and using a mortgage with which to buy the property. Consider a notional £200,000 value of property and we are a savvy investor who managed to negotiate a reduction on its £200,000 price to £150,000, so a 25% discount to true market value. This might not have been easy and we might have had to view say 15 similar properties and offer the discounted amount on each until we came across someone needing to sell quickly who accepted our offer.

We can then buy this with a mortgage and just put 25% down as a deposit at £37,500. We could also use cash, if we had it, to buy the property outright and then still remortgage six months later on to get all our capital back out. As will be explained later, it is still termed a remortgage if we buy with cash and take a mortgage loan on the property later.

Anyway, let us stick with a mortgage purchase example and say we then did some work and spent another £10,000 on it by fitting a new kitchen and bathroom and doing some general decoration upgrade work. This then raised the perceived value by another £30,000 say. So the property is now valued at an open market valuation of £230,000. However, we have only spent a total of just £160,000 on it.

After six months, we decide to remortgage the property to recognise its true value and take a 75% LTV mortgage against it. In this case that will be 75% of £230,000 which is £172,500. This is £12,500 more than was put in, and we could release all of this. This is, of course, providing the Valuer agrees with that valuation, and the rental valuation passes the lender's stress testing calculation. Normally, however, we would be happy just to take out what we had put in, or as close as we can to it.

These percentages also work with lower value properties, in case you are in the North of England, where you can even buy reasonable properties at discount - around £50,000 at the time of writing. Say I spend quite some time viewing and offering on properties and manage to buy at discount to true market value at £50,000 meaning the property would normally sell at £67,000 (approximately a 25% reduction). I then spent £3,000 to add a perceived value of about £10,000, meaning the property can now be valued at around £77,000.

After six months, I then remortgage with a 75% LTV mortgage and this gives me a mortgage loan value of £57,750 which again is more than what I have actually invested in the property. At the remortgage, I can get my full deposit amount back plus some money to cover mortgaging and remortgaging expenses meaning I own the property using 100% finance, and therefore none of my money down on the deal. I can then repeat this as many times as I want, to build up my portfolio with No Money Down (NMD) or No Money Left In (NMLI) as some investors more accurately prefer to call it.

However, remember what I said about profitability, we still need to service the loan and manage other property costs, which we need to be able to do from the rental income, otherwise, we are storing up trouble for ourselves later. I should know because that is exactly what I did when I started. I was buying one after another for effective 100% financing and then suddenly realised how hard it was to keep up the mortgage payments and cover maintenance costs. I then had to work on how to maximise rental income, but that is another story.

The moral of that story is however to make sure you can afford the mortgage and maintenance costs. As covered in the last section on Profitability Calculations. Additionally, allow for the fact that rental income is not a given and you have to have someone in your property happy and able to pay you the rent each and every month. Keeping your properties occupied with paying tenants then becomes a key activity, as we will come on to in later chapters.

Ownership (Personal or Company)

Until recently, it did not matter too much whether you owned property in your own name or in a company name. The general advice for tax reasons used to be to own it in your personal name. Also, the mortgages for personal ownership in the past had better rates than for company mortgages.

Enter a certain Chancellor called George Osborne and all this changed overnight. The budget he presented shocked the UK property investing world as he effectively disallowed mortgage payments as a business expense for people owning investment property in their own name. He replaced this with a tax credit of 20% of the value of the interest paid. The net effect was to financially punish any landlords holding properties in their own name and who were in the higher rate tax bracket.

To add insult to injury, he further stipulated that the fictitious profits which this creates are to be added to a person's income for tax banding calculations. That meant that those who earned in the basic rate of tax, as well as invested in a small number of BTL properties, could easily be pushed into the higher rate tax bracket. This is simply due to that tax legislation change, often termed the Section 24 tax rule, or more often expressed disparagingly as the anti-landlord tax.

Mainly because of this reason, most new investors set up a limited company in which they can buy their investment properties. In a company, you can still claim 100% of your interest payment as an expense against your property business. You should therefore take professional tax advice on your specific situation and property intentions. However, you will likely be told to form a limited company and buy properties inside of that company

How to Buy

There are many ways to find investment property to buy. Here we cover the main ones that you should consider as a BRRRR property investor, together with a few tips and comments about each approach. Having several of these routes to gaining property purchasing opportunities is advisable, although focusing on one in particular is the best approach so you can to build up focussed experience and relevant business contacts quickly.

The most common way that property investors buy property is the conventional way that most of us will look for our own residential property to buy to live in. This is through the high street estate agents. Most agents are now presenting their offerings online with the major internet property portals that you will already be aware of. There is however no substitute for walking into the offices of the estate agents and making direct personal contact. Let the agents behind the desks know what you are looking for and ask them to contact you if something comes along.

Don't expect them to do that however on the first request, or even after several such same requests. It takes time for them to get to know you and take you seriously. It is very likely they will see you as a possible time-waster, especially if you have not purchased from them already. How many would-be investors do you think they come across every month? New faces all saying the same thing about their property investing ambitions.

Estate agents want to be able to sell property quickly and a hesitant new property investor might not fit that requirements bill. If they are selling to new investors then there is a higher chance that such people might back out of the deal, which puts them back to square one again with that sale. There are often no upfront deposit requirements on property sales, therefore agents will see this as a real risk they have to face with new investors.

Even if you can tell them that you are actively investing, how can they know for sure? Well, one way is that you religiously show up in their offices looking for properties for sale, week after week. If you can't make it into the agency then you will be calling them by phone instead. You need to put your name and your specific kind of property you are looking for clearly in their mind. Repetition is what will do this. It will also underline that you are serious by the amount of time you are spending in making repeat contact with them.

Having one person as the main point of contact in each agent's office is the best way to do this. Aim to make contact with the most senior person in the office that is in a role that is customer-facing. This will likely be the agency owner, the Office Manager, or maybe even the Valuer. It will differ from agency to agency. In the past, I have dealt with the more junior office staff as well, which can work out satisfactorily, but it is better to aim higher up the organisation if you can.

Another thing about dealing solely with the more junior staff is that you will likely see a higher turnover rate with them. This means you spend a lot of time getting to know them and getting them to know what you are looking for only to find when you go into the office the next time, they have left for another job somewhere else. If you are fortunate enough, they will have just gone to work for another agency in the same area. But don't count on it, try to hit as high as possible in the organisation as they are the most influential and most stable staff there is.

Once you do start to make purchases through the agents, it is very likely they will start calling you when deals come in. They will do this as soon as something comes on their books which they believe will be of interest to you. As you get to know them even better, they will call you as something is coming through but not officially available yet (when they don't even have the brochure signed off by the vendor).

In this way, you will be ahead of the crowd of most other investors looking for deals. This is the position you want to be in with the agents in the area you invest in. But don't expect that to happen overnight, it could take a year or more even with focussed attention on this matter with them, as well as making actual property purchases (either with them or with other agents).

I have found the estate agency business to be quite incestuous and therefore if you start buying as an investor in one particular local market, it won't be long before your name and reputation get around. Make sure you make a good impression, that will open up more buying opportunities for you without you even trying.

Buying Direct to Vendor, as it is known, simply means dealing directly with the seller without an agent involved and has been the cornerstone of many BRRRR investors. You might see Direct to Vendor colloquially abbreviated to D2V in property-related communications, such as email or on property forums and some property books.

Although you can get some good deals from estate agents, always remember that they are representing the seller and trying to get the best deal for them, not for you first and foremost. You are simply a means to them achieving this. Agents will also be taking a commission on the purchase which means you will be partly paying for their service.

However, the vendor will only accept an offer that looks good to them after such costs are deducted from the offer price. Therefore, you will have to offer at least a little higher when purchasing through an agent compared to dealing with a vendor direct.

Going Direct to Vendor is then likely to yield you cheaper properties. You can often see boards outside properties which is stating it is For Sale by Owner, or words to that effect. These are worth enquiring about, but maybe not likely where you will get the best Direct to Vendor deals. In these cases, it is more likely they are just trying to avoid the costs of the selling agent to make a little more money, but also likely they have had the properties valued beforehand by estate agents.

These valuations will be 'aspirational valuations' aimed more at an agent securing the vendor's custom by giving them an attractive sales price. It depends on the market at the time and the competition between agents, but typically these can be priced around 10% higher than what the agent thinks it will sell for in reality. Of course, in very hot markets, sales prices can go above the asking price, but normally it is the case that properties are advertised with a slight overpricing.

You therefore need to find another way to go direct to the vendors. You are looking to find people where the actual sale of the property is more important than them getting the absolute best price for it. This is not taking advantage of people, but helping them out and giving them what they need. You can only guess at the reasons as it is very likely they won't say why. In extreme cases, people might need to sell quickly to avoid repossession or avoid bankruptcy. I have come across both of these in my investing activity (in both of these cases, I only found out after agreeing on the purchase).

If you can deliver on a fast sale, direct with the seller, you can therefore get the property at a price that is below the actual market value for the property. The normal market value is often taken as a price that would result in an expected sale after 6 – 8 weeks of marketing. Getting properties at these prices is what is known as buying Below Market Value (BMV). Whilst this is also possible with estate agents, it is more likely with deals direct to vendor, especially if you are acquiring these leads by advertising and offering quick sales.

The question remains as to how best to get these deals. The way from the past, and still a technique used today, is to leaflet the area you want to buy in. You can do this yourself or via a leafleting agent that sells this service at a price per thousand delivered. Of course, the response rate is very low, but you don't need very many responses to be able to cover the leafleting costs.

Another advantage of this approach is that you can laser focus on the neighbourhoods you want to buy in. These are where you have identified that the typical purchase prices and the rental values are at the right levels to make the deals work. These areas should also suit the type of tenant you are aiming for when you come to let out the property.

This is therefore better than going to estate agents where they are likely to give you all the deals available in all the areas they cover, just in case they can attract you and make a sale. That is of course most probably going to be a waste of time for both of you, but they are not likely to be able to appreciate that. You can mix these two approaches of course, and get the best of both lead-generating methods. These go well together as you focus in on your target areas. You may have heard some term your target area your 'Goldmine Area', simply because this is the area where you make the money.

In addition to the core leafleting activity in the area you want to invest in to attract potential sales leads, you can also publicise what you are looking for in other ways. These other ways include posting up advertising cards in local shops, putting signs on parked vehicles (vehicles you own!), using local billboard advertising if available (which can be expensive), offering financial incentives for anyone who brings a deal to you that goes ahead (by paying them a so-called finder's fee).

A modern twist on this approach of advertising to the specific areas you want to invest in is the use of Facebook adverts. It is now possible to target people using postcodes so that only people who live in the postcodes you state on the advert will see the advert come up on their Facebook newsfeed.

It can take quite some learning to use Facebook adverts in this way but it is not too difficult and well-worth learning how to do it. Budgets can start quite low as you are not needing to target many people. This however is a whole topic in its own right, but I just give you a summary flavour for the possibility here.

A spin-off from the Direct to Vendor approach, is the wholesaling of such deals by so-called Property Sourcers. Typically, these property sourcers specialise in obtaining BMV deals and putting these out on offer on their websites for people to purchase. You can either purchase a lead (with no guarantee of a sale but at a low cost), or work on the basis of paying a success fee for an actual purchase facilitated through them (typically a percentage fee akin to an estate agent, but usually a little higher).

Some of the property sourcers operate more like national estate agents who put you in touch with the local vendor. It is therefore worth registering with such services if they can offer you deals in your area. I have seen some very good deals from these services, at least as good as could have been obtained using other direct-to-vendor methods. This is because they are advertising for motivated sellers that want to sell fast for a lower price than they could otherwise achieve.

It is worth making mention of another traditional source of BMV deals, which are an essential component part of the BRRRR investment strategy, and that is of buying at auction. The caveat with this approach is that it can be quite risky and better left until you have more property experience under your belt. In addition, the financing of these auction deals is more time-critical and there are severe penalties if you fail to purchase in time. Stipulated purchase lead times can vary typically from just 14 days to 28 days.

Therefore, buying at auction is not something that I would recommend as a starting strategy, but more one for when you become more cash-rich (with cash in the bank) and can find some good deals taking the auction route. Don't take it as read that you will get the best deals at auction, as sometimes you can be buying a liability or paying well over the market value in a heated auction room with a buying frenzy. I have witnessed both of these, but fortunate enough not to be caught still in the running when the hammer went down.

Property Types

The property type you focus on will be a part of your investing strategy. This might well be affected by your selected tenant type, but there can be some crossover between property types and different kinds of tenants in some cases.

The basic types of property you will come across in property investing in the UK are terraced houses (usually dating from around 1900), semi-detached (usually ex local authority housing stock), detached houses (usually used for higher-yielding HMOs), and flats either in small units or in apartment blocks (flats in apartment blocks are often more suitable as professional lets).

For the BRRRR strategy, it is often the terraced houses and semi-detached houses that are targeted. This is due to both their lower initial cost and also the opportunity to increase the property value sufficiently to refinance the investment capital back out. Detached houses are sometimes also possible but in combination with the conversion of residential houses to Houses in Multiple Occupation (HMOs).

Tenant Types

There are several basic categories of tenant types that you will need to consider, in combination with the kind of property you choose to invest in and the areas in which you choose to buy. These three factors make up your focus for property investment. When it comes to tenant type you will need to be comfortable that you are interested in that sector of property rentals. Or if not, then you need to be well connected with someone who is able to manage those tenants for you.

The first tenant type to consider is those claiming social benefits. These can be long-term unemployed and this also includes single parents who claim child benefit payments. Included in this sector are those with disability allowances. These are all tenants that will be getting income without working. These tenant types are certainly not without challenges. Although it can be a good rental sector to be involved with if you can manage the details around it and ensure that you receive the rental payments.

However, this sector has been quite challenging recently with the changes made regarding the introduction of Universal Credit (UC). This is where the tenants get paid a single payment each month and have to budget to live on that for a whole month. If they do fall behind on rent payments, as is often the case in my experience, you can apply to the Department for Work and Pensions (DWP) to have the rent paid directly to you. To do this you have to fill in a UC47 form that is available on the Government website, and fill in the necessary details.

Also in my experience, considerable property wear and tear as well as accidental and/or deliberate damage is quite often associated with these kinds of lettings, so you will need to account for that in your costs model for lettings profitability projections.

Blue Collar workers are another tenant type that sometimes occupies the same kinds of houses as the social benefits claimants. With these workers, you can get interruptions in rental income when they lose their work or move from one job to another. Again, in my experience, the rent will not often be paid if they have other payment obligations at these times. You will need to arrange for them to catch up with their rent payments before they get too far behind.

Public Sector workers are similar to blue-collar workers as tenants but will be a little more stable in their work and their ability to regularly pay their rent.

Student lets are quite an industry in areas where students coming from afar are looking for local digs. That all changed all of a sudden when Covid-19 hit of course. But when things are normal, students do give you a surety of tenancy for a full academic year at least. You do also have the chance of getting the council tax paid by virtue of the tenants claiming for this relief upon occupation. This is easier said than done but is achievable if you set out to do exactly that by making it chargeable to them if they don't get their council tax relief awarded.

The above last three tenant types might also occupy HMOs as they are often single and without children to look after. In some cases, you will find some of your HMO tenants will ask for houses for themselves as they seek to get more established and maybe start a family.

Professional people include those with higher-paid jobs that are looking for higher-end properties. These can typically be apartments in apartment blocks, often near town or city centres close to where they work. The rent payments from these people are generally much less problematic and they tend to keep the property in good order in my experience.

The above are however somewhat very general statements, and you will develop your own sense of awareness of the different kinds of tenants that you would be comfortable serving. In the end, you will need to select one or two that match your investment property type and location where the figures add up and the rental income will enable you to run your property business at a profit.

Knowing Your Market

We have already touched on what is commonly known in property investing as your goldmine area. This concerns the location of the type of property that you have decided to invest in as your main focus. This location is often down to a part of a town or even to a set of streets in a particular area. Or it could be as wide as a whole municipality, in which you seek a particular type of property to invest in.

For some investors, this will simply be their local town or city, or maybe the next town or city from where they live. These housing market locations are ideal because they are literally on your doorstep. However, to be a so-called goldmine area, the investing numbers have to add up to make sense to invest in the first place. You would do well to find these areas as close as possible to where you live, as this will make doing deals and later managing properties much easier for you.

If you are not in such a fortunate position to have something local that you can focus on as your market, or goldmine area, you may well need to look further afield. Investing in markets that are remote from where you live brings additional challenges. In some cases, I have known people come to live in the area where they invest during the week, then go home for the weekend. In other examples, I know of people simply using local property agents to find, refurbish and manage their properties.

However, no matter where your market is, you need to get to know it very well. You will need to become acquainted with the street names, and even which part of the street. There are many examples I can think of where it is better to buy on one part of a street than another part. However, the prices of the properties on these two parts of the street would not give anything away that one part is better to buy in than the other.

In relation to the property prices in your market area, you will need to be up to date as to at least what the asking prices are. This is so you can spot a bargain when you see one and can act quickly. Depending on the area and depending on the stage in the property cycle, selling prices could be less, roughly the same or higher than asking prices. This is something you should also be sensitive to in order to put in offers that reflect the state of the market.

To get a feel for the prices and the areas, you will need to look at all the properties that are being sold and what prices they are being advertised for. You need to account for the condition of the property when it is being sold of course. The condition of the property often determines the minimum and maximum of the selling prices respectively.

These minimums and maximums present useful information for BRRRR. You should be aiming to buy below the normal minimum (allowing for condition) and looking to refurbish to a standard that can command the highest sale price. Even though you will not be selling, the selling prices will be what the Valuer will be using to base their remortgage valuation on when you come to refinance.

The lower you can buy the property for, the more headroom you will have to add value and increase the property valuation ready for refinancing. It is not just a matter of spotting the properties that require the most work, but rather the ones that you can add value to for the minimum amount of work. You cannot hold out for the most idealistic of these situations however, you will have to buy at some stage and you need to buy the best you can at the time you need to buy.

By way of example, I have bought properties that I would not exactly say were at the bottom of the valuation range for the area I was investing in. However, they were only looking run down due to cosmetics and a small change such as changing out the sanitary ware, painting throughout, and putting in new floor coverings would raise appearance massively. Therefore, this required very little money being put in, to create a nice and attractive living space.

On the other hand, I have bought properties that were stripped bare and still stank of urine. You can guess that I got these at good prices, although the amount of refurbishment work required would be much more substantial. This means the costs going in are much higher to put the property into a rentable state, as well as one that will value up well on revaluation after the works have been done.

Getting back to the original theme of this section of the book, you need to be able to have a good feel for property prices for all range of locations you invest in as well as the condition of the property. Having a feel for what it would cost to do up the property and what it would be worth when that work is done is also a very valuable skill to have. These can however only come with experience, although you could get a kickstart from someone who knows the area and are happy to work with you on all of this.

Buying BMV

We have already touched on the need to buy BMV. Here we look at situations that indicate what is likely to be an opportunity to purchase such a below market value property. I was taught this on property courses in my very early days of investing. These were taught as the 5 D's, although I have seen different words for each D from different people. What does not change however are the two top D's in my experience, these are Death and Divorce.

There is certainly no shortage of these two situations and in each case, there is a desire to sell quickly. When I am viewing a property, I am always trying to find out what is the real reason for the sale. I simply ask the agent, or even the seller if they are present, although don't always expect the correct answer all the time. But it is worth simply asking in case you do get the information you require.

Once you know the reason for the sale you can maybe think about how best to be able to frame your offer. However, in most cases, it will likely mean they want a quick sale and hopefully not for the full market value. The only time that this is required when someone is in a desperate situation is when someone is in negative equity. In that case, it will be hard to do a good deal that works for both of you. There are things you can do but not in line with the BRRRR approach which we are focussed on here.

The people in this situation can only hope for someone to come along and offer the price they need to clear the mortgage balance. Or otherwise, help them with the mortgage situation such as maybe via lease options arrangements, but that is beyond the scope and topic of this book on BRRRR.

One common need to sell quickly is when there is a threat of repossession because they could not afford to pay the monthly mortgage payments for some time. Loss of a job is the most likely reason for this, and they therefore need to sell quickly to remove their mortgage payment obligations they can no longer satisfy. If they don't sell and repossession takes place, they will likely be worse off than if they had sold it themselves.

Once repossession has actually taken place with some unfortunate souls, there is still an opportunity to buy at a good price compared to normal market value. However, although I have bought repossessed property, I have also lost a few of these deals because the property is kept on the market until you exchange contracts. It is therefore best to look at these if you are in a cash buying situation, or you risk losing several thousand by starting the purchase process with a mortgage, only to be outbid on price at the last moment. The problem with buying with a mortgage is that, after the mortgage valuation has been done, you can't simply increase the offered price to respond to a counter bid. The deal then falls through and you lose your money invested to date.

Whatever the reason, you are looking to buy at a price that is well below market value. If you aim for 25% below then that would be a good figure to aim for. The larger you make this discount figure, the more difficult it will be to find the properties where such a discount will be acceptable. This means you have more leg work to do by viewing more properties and putting in more offers.

I was always taught that this is simply a numbers game in that the more properties you view and offer on, the more likely it is that you will get a low offer accepted. It is just a matter of dropping on the right situation where you have that motivated seller just wanting to offload the property as soon as possible.

Therefore, be prepared to do a lot of work on this front if you want the very best deals. If you relax your buying discount figure you can of course get more offers accepted, but these might not quite stack up for the BRRRR system.

Adding Value

This is another subject we have already touched upon. You can start to see how a lot of what we discuss here is interrelated, and that very much is the case. I am trying to discuss each component part of the BRRRR process separately, but in reality, they are very much all interconnected.

When you are adding value to a property to increase its valuation, you are creating what is known as forced appreciation. This is as opposed to waiting for the general market to appreciate in value over time due to property price rises. The reason we need to use forced appreciation in BRRRR is that we need that higher valuation quickly. This is so we can release the money invested in the property and move on to the next project with it.

In BRRRR, adding value is all about creating that uplift in valuation from what you purchased the property at to what a valuer will value it up at on a remortgage. Note that this is not the selling price, although these should in theory be the same. You have to account for the sentiment of the mortgage valuers at the time. I have known valuers who have valued over typical market values in times of rapidly rising markets, then value well below in times of housing market difficulty.

A valuer wants to make sure they do not get caught in a situation where they have been found to have overvalued a property. Instead, valuers would rather be on the safe side and that tends to be what dictates how they value. It can also be a personal matter, which we cannot control, and you are at the whim of their feelings to some extent. What you get from them as a valuation is what the mortgage company or bank will go by and you will not easily be able to change that, if at all.

It is therefore best to make changes to a property that you can demonstrate you have done enough work to justify the increase in valuation you are seeking. You would do well to keep copies of receipts for materials and work to substantiate this claim for the increase in value. The more of a light refurbishment you do the more likely it will be that you will not be granted a substantial increase in valuation, especially if you are remortgaging inside a year of the actual property purchase.

The longer the time goes by from the original purchase, the less the Valuer will be influenced by the improvement work and the more of an independent assessment they will make. In BRRRR however, we are needing to get a revaluation to the highest possible level as soon as possible, therefore it is better to take on projects where you can more easily demonstrate an increase in value, as well as significant work input to achieve it.

You need to look out for these opportunities before you purchase. When you find a candidate property where you can likely add a lot of value for the minimum amount of expenditure, you need to try your best to purchase that property. Although don't be tempted to offer above the amount you need to buy for to make the revaluation calculations work, or at least be as close that as you are satisfied (discussed later).

You will be right to be thinking just what are these opportunities? I will give you some typical examples of what I look out for, which are the more common and obvious ones. Although these may not be obvious to some people and therefore it becomes your advantage if you can spot things that others do not see as such opportunities. You should always be viewing properties with the eyes of what is possible, not just what is in front of you.

Now for the examples. The top of the list for me is to make another bedroom. One area I find gets overlooked in traditional rental housing stock, like terraced houses, is when the attic has a single bedroom. It is often possible to make that space into two single bedrooms by splitting it near the middle of the space, then going all the way back into the eves with each bedroom created. Quite often the existing attic bedroom will have fairly high false walls that can be knocked through, then taken back to much smaller dwarf walls, just before the eves.

In these cases, you need to know that the attic floor has been properly converted already, this is to take the weight needed to be used as a dwelling room floor, and not just as a loft space. You can have this checked by a survey if you are not sure. Or maybe the seller has a building regulations certificate for the conversion work. Even if that is not the case you can always change the floor, albeit a fairly large job. The last one I did like that was very dirty as well and caused major disruption to the other refurbishment work taking place in the house.

There are other more simple ways to create an extra bedroom. If you have an oversized large double bedroom, you can maybe split that into two singles. However, you need to make sure the house still has a double bedroom. There is no point making single bedrooms that are too small either, it will more likely have a devaluing effect. Believe me, I have made that mistake, not to be repeated.

But where you can split a room to make two decent-sized rooms, it is only a case normally of a partition wall and fitting a door or two. As long as you install good sound insulation on the partition wall and it is thick enough so that it will comply with building regulations. Essentially this is just plasterboard on either side of wooden posts with sound insulation wool sandwiched in the middle. When painted up and serving to make the two rooms out of one, you can make a much larger increase in value than the work would have cost you. The only other requirement is an outside window for each room so you might need to add a window as well.

Adding an ensuite to a double bedroom will have a notable increase in the value of a house. These are fairly easy to do as long as the bedroom is large enough and you can locate the ensuite in a convenient place in the room. The key thing to look out for here is where do you put the drainage pipe for the sanitary ware. This can be affected by the direction the joists run as well as where the main foul drainage pipe is that you need to connect into. You can always run it above the floorboard and enclose in boxing, but that is not the neatest of jobs.

Creative things can be done with bathrooms and ensuites in any location, even if the drainage is a seemingly insurmountable problem. This is because you can use an electrically driven macerator and smallbore pipes which can also pump upwards a certain amount if required. For example, with a toilet, you might want to locate it in a basement space, where the external drainage system will likely be at a higher level than the sanitary fittings. However, I don't like to use those for rental properties as it is easy for someone to put something down the toilet which damages the macerator. For me, this is a last resort, although I have used them on two occasions. I have also had the associated problems with them that I just described too.

On the topic of bathrooms and ensuites, it is important to know that building regulations only require ventilation and not necessarily natural light in these rooms. This means you have more flexibility on where these rooms are located. This is as opposed to bedroom creation where you need natural light in the form of a window that can also be opened for ventilation. For a toilet situation, the ventilation can come from a forced fan air duct that extracts from the toilet area. There are building regulations around this, but that is nothing that an electrician cannot accommodate.

As a general rule, correcting any small room sizing problem, by maybe removing a wall or relocating walls, is another easy value-raising exercise. For example, if the kitchen is notably too small, you can maybe spot how you can correct that. This might be in the case where there is a so-called galley kitchen that is located in something more akin to a corridor than a room. You can even relocate kitchens to other rooms simply by installing the kitchen units and appliances in another location.

Other changes you can make are the more well-known ones where you simply change out tired kitchen units or change the bathroom suite. Removing (or skimming over) any old design of Artex will also help, and this can be on walls or ceilings. Any uneven or pitted walls can be skimmed over or replastered entirely if the underlying plaster has lost its bonding to the wall. Removing wallpaper and creating freshly skimmed plaster walls to paint over creates a much better appearance for a little additional investment.

Replacing internal doors is another quick win area, where the doors are in desperate need of upgrading. External door replacement can also have an instant impact if you can install a better door and give the house more curb appeal. As does fitting new uPVC windows where the ones installed are very old or even of the original wooden single glazing type.

The list can go on, but those items are the top ones that I have used over the years. You might find other nice little tips and tricks to improve the value as you go about your property business. When you do, be sure to add these to your arsenal of value-raising opportunities that you look for when you go out and view properties.

Initial Capital Raising

The minimum amount of money you will normally need to buy a property is the amount of deposit money required for the mortgage. The balance of the payment will then come from the payment by the mortgage company for you to buy the property. In addition to the deposit, you will need some money for other solicitor's completion costs and Stamp Duty Land Tax (SDLT) as appropriate, but the main amount of money will still be the deposit payment.

There are various ways to raise this money but the mortgaging company or bank will be very interested and ask how you got that money. They would prefer to hear and see demonstrated that it is simply from personal savings. Other forms of conventional capital raising may be acceptable, such as by remortgaging your residential property to release equity, but that may depend on the lender.

What they would not want to hear is that you have loaned it from someone else or that you took cash from a credit card or any other lending facility. Anything which means you are 100% financing the property with loaned money is a red light to them, they will likely refuse any mortgage application where they even suspect this to be the case. You therefore need to be careful and clear about this matter in your mortgage application and leave no room for any doubt about the legitimacy of the deposit money, according to their criteria.

There is nothing to stop you however from making a joint mortgage application with someone who has the money for the deposit. You can then buy the property together and have a separate agreement with them as to how they benefit from their shared investment. This could be a share of rental income and/or equity in the property. The amount of percentage share is totally up to you and them to agree upon. I would say this should be avoided if possible, however, as personalities can complicate matters, but if you have no other option, you will need to take such extra steps to at least get started on the property investment ladder.

Assuming you did have someone help you with the property purchase, you could then pay them back when you refinance the property later after you have added value to it and increased the property valuation. That may then enable you to take full ownership by paying them off the deposit amount that they first put in. If you do get into these situations, it is best to involve close family members if you can to reduce the risk of problems. Although going out to others can be done and this is often known as a joint venture.

It would be wise to get everything down in writing regarding any joint venture or family deals that you do. This will reduce the chances of misunderstandings and fall-outs over the details of such matters later. You can involve a solicitor in this to advise and then they can produce formal documentation which will also cover you for unexpected situations later, such as death and other lesser matters.

I have always preferred to raise my own investment capital to avoid the need to call on other people, that is just my preference. You may prefer to work with others who have the money and want to invest with you. When you do it that way, you may then have none of your money in a deal, but you do have to manage your investors and you will still have liabilities you will need to settle later.

You can also sell any assets you might have that are no longer required, or paper assets such as stocks and shares if you have any. Any conventional methods of raising money by disposal of personal assets will be acceptable as a deposit for a property of course.

There may be some more creative ways of raising the deposit finance but be careful if you take that route, this is in case it is found to be not acceptable to the lender. Discuss any of the approaches you may be considering with your mortgage broker and they will be able to advise what is acceptable and what is not. In some cases, as already stated, it might depend on a particular lender as to whether it is acceptable or not.

Buying With, or Without Finance

You do not have to use mortgage finance to purchase an investment property. This even applies to a situation where you are intending to remortgage the property and release most of the equity. This is the equity you will have built up by forced appreciation arising from the improvement works.

The term remortgage is therefore a little misleading. I have known this even confuses some of the leading recognised commentators in the property business. Admittedly it does rather seem to imply you need a mortgage in place in order to remortgage and switch to a different mortgage. However, you can remortgage after a cash purchase and you will need a specific remortgage finance product to do this with. In technical terms, if you own an unencumbered property (i.e. one you do not have any loans secured against), or you can remortgage to release any capital and equity tied up in it (less the value of the deposit amount required for the lender's security for the remortgage).

More simply stated, you can use a remortgage product to replace an existing mortgage or take a mortgage loan out on a property you own that has no first charge registered against it. This will most likely be because you bought it for cash, but it could be because you inherited it, or already paid off the loan capital.

In BRRRR, this means that you can buy a property for cash and still use a remortgage product later to release the money you put into it, and only leave enough equity behind that is required as a minimum to act as an effective deposit for the remortgage product.

You might wonder why you would want to buy with cash rather than with a mortgage in BRRRR in any case. That would be a good line of thinking and worthy of discussion. In my property investing ventures I have done both. If I had the cash in the bank that could support an outright purchase, I would use that (even though that case might have come from an equity release by remortgaging my residential home in the first place).

The reason I would use the cash in the bank is that it is powerfully attractive to show an estate agent or a seller that you have the money there sitting ready to make payment for a property. It might well put you ahead in the queue for the purchase of a property where others are proposing to use mortgages to make the purchase. This is because a mortgage offer can always fall through, whereas cash in the bank is not going to disappear as easily as a mortgage offer could. Such as in the case that someone did not meet the mortgage criteria during the mortgage application process.

However, buying with a mortgage is appropriate if you can only raise the deposit money for the purchase. It will work out a little more expensive as you will have to pay for mortgage-related legal fees and the lender's upfront fees, as well as property purchase fees. It can also tie you in with early redemption penalties if you change your mortgage before a certain time stated.

Some brokers or financial advisers will argue that mortgages are intended for longer-term investment, adding that you will be abusing the system by using these for short-term loans by remortgaging after a few years. I do not take this view and find this is often espoused by those who want to sell you the more expensive bridging loans instead, which are only provided as short-term products. Consult a few mortgage brokers on this matter to get a balanced opinion of your particular situation and intentions.

On balance, therefore, I prefer to purchase with cash and remortgage later. This is ideal for BRRRR but not necessary as you can take out other borrowings to cover you for the period while you are carrying out the refurbishment work. These can be mortgages where the mortgage broker is aware of your intention to switch to a different mortgage product later, or even an expensive bridging loan if necessary (depending on the condition of the property and whether it is in a mortgageable condition at purchase).

In either case, you will just need to be sure that the costs of the finance being used do not affect you too badly. If it does then you need to get the properties for less money than you are currently offering. You need to cover the costs of the finance (monthly payments and any entry and exit fees) as well as the costs of the refurbishment work as it all comes from the same pot. If this is not possible then you will have to settle for as close as you can get and then use the rental profits to repay the capital you cannot extract by the refinance.

Refurbishment Mortgages

Refurbishment mortgages are intended to help with the situation described above. These mortgages allow you to release equity without needing to remortgage whilst also knowing what capital will be advanced to you on completion of the works. The idea behind these mortgages is that the Valuer is instructed to assess the refurbishment work that you intend to do and estimate what additional value that will create for the property. The full amount of mortgage money is then approved at application, but an amount relating to the additional value you are to create is held on account until the work is done.

When you have done the refurbishment work, the Valuer is then instructed to revalue the property and verify the work has been done as per the original description and to the required quality level. Once this has been verified in a revaluation report, which you will have to pay for, the retained amount of money is released to your bank account. It will then immediately be added to your mortgage loan balance secured against the property. Hence the monthly interest payments increase accordingly and you get the capital released to you straight away.

On the face of it, these mortgage products would seem ideal for BRRRR. The issue is that the amount the lender will agree to advance after the refurbishment work is more likely to add up to around the amount of money spent on the refurbishment alone. This means your original deposit payment is still locked away as equity in the property. In most cases, there is simply a maximum amount that they will be prepared to advance to you after the work. This typically could be of the order of just £20,000.

Refurbishment mortgages are a good way of getting capital released quickly because you get it back as soon as you have completed the work. There is no waiting for the normally required six months before a remortgage will be considered. If a two-stage approach to the release of your capital will work for you, then you can consider this approach. However, it somewhat complicates BRRRR and causes refinancing delays as Refurbishment Products may also carry significant early redemption penalties.

I have used refurbishment mortgages before on several projects. However, this was at a later stage in my property investing ventures when I could slow down a little and still be content to delay the return of my capital without hampering progress on other projects. The refurbishment products I took out had redemption penalties until just at the end of a two-year period. I remortgaged after those two years and pulled out the additional amount of invested capital.

RICS Surveys

The first step in the formal mortgage or remortgage application process is the valuation of the property. In fact, at the time that you apply for a mortgage, you will also likely be required to pay for the mortgage valuation upfront. These will need to be carried out by a Royal Institute of Chartered Surveyors (RICS) registered surveyor. However, the lender will be arranging for this to be done.

After paying for the valuation survey, you will need to supply some contact details for access to the property and this can be either you if it is a remortgage, or the selling agent if you are buying a property. Probably during the same week either you or the selling agents, as appropriate, will be contacted to arrange the date and time of the valuation.

When the surveyor arrives at the property, notes will be taken on its construction and condition and some key measurements made. This normally does not take very long as it is not an in-depth survey, just a valuation for the purpose of remortgaging. Some of the work will already have been done or will be done later, by using online information to help assess the property value and rental value.

The report is then written up and sent to the lender. Then a copy is often forwarded to your mortgage broker from the lender, and probably a copy sent to you. Even though you are likely to have paid for the survey it is not really for you but the lender. Often you get a copy out of courtesy, although it is not a contractual requirement that you get a copy.

The most important results are of course the property valuation figure and the rental income assessment. However, it is worth reading the report in full to check for any other comments that can be of interest to you. Specifically, check whether there are any recommendations or requirements for any essential works to be done.

Sometimes the Valuer will insist that certain works are done for the valuation to stand, which is a requirement and therefore becomes a condition of mortgaging. Sometimes the Valuer will just recommend that certain works are done and this may then not be part of any condition for mortgaging, simply advisory. These issues appear in a general comments section of the report, which is often the most verbose part of what is normally a check-box and facts entry short report.

In some cases, the surveyor will list some works that are essential and need to be done after mortgaging. They will assign an appropriate amount of money the lender should hold back from the agreed loan amount, this is called a retention. This money is then released for you later when the remedial work has been completed.

In this case, you will have to put more of your own money into the property and then claim it back later when you have had the work done. This will require a check made by the Valuer that the corrective work has been done to a satisfactory standard.

To get the release of the retention money, this will require another visit from the Valuer, for which there will be an additional charge. This charge will however not be as much as the original valuation cost since there will be less work to do in terms of reporting and assessment. Sometimes, it may be sufficient to supply a certificate to prove the requirements have been met, it all depends on what the issue concerning the retention is about.

By planning to get the retention issue dealt with as soon as possible, you can get the full amount of mortgage drawdown money completed quickly. If you are remortgaging, it may be possible to deal with any such issue before the completion of the mortgage, meaning you can get the full drawdown from day one of the new mortgage.

It is important however to realise that if you want a detailed assessment of the true condition of a property to be purchased, you will need to have a separate survey done, which is at least at the level of what is termed a *Homebuyer Report*, previously known as a *Homebuyer's Survey*. For a more in-depth survey, and a more expensive one, you can get a *Building Survey* done, this was previously known as a *Structural Survey*. Both of these types of surveys have to be carried out by an RICS qualified surveyor and so done to a professional standard.

A more detailed building survey is not likely to be required unless the property is very old or unique. However, the lender's mortgage valuation report will simply not go into the level of detail required to give you full confidence in the condition of the property you are buying. The Homebuyer Report will usually be at the right level for most property purchases. These surveys can be carried out on either buy-to-let or residential property purchases as they are looking for the same issues generally associated with a property.

You might find it strange that the lender is happy with the least detailed report of all. You would think that the lender would be interested in knowing as much as possible about the property they are lending against. However, they have found the basic valuation report adequate for protecting them sufficiently for their lending business.

Of course, they have an additional level of security, which is you who owns the property. Therefore, they can expect that in most cases, where there are things that have gone unnoticed by the valuation report, these will be addressed later by the property owner. A property repossession rarely takes place very quickly after purchase, so they see this as another level of protection regarding the condition of the property they are securing the loan against.

Besides, if they have to sell at less than the mortgage value for some valid reason, they can still chase the ex-owner for the difference in money between what it sold for and what they owed them.

The Homebuyer Report or a Building Survey is not at all necessary for your protection in the case of a remortgage, as you already own the property and there is no further risk to mitigate. In this case, the lender's mortgage valuation report alone is fine of course. On occasions though, depending on the property, the lender might insist on a Building Survey, which you would have to pay for.

However, in the case of a purchase, all this responsibility is falling on you so it is wise to understand that the valuation survey is not to be fully relied upon as far as you are concerned. Getting a more detailed survey, privately commissioned by you, is a wise thing to do although not necessary for mortgaging purposes. When I first started investing in residential property, I would always get a Homebuyers Survey done (now called a Homebuyer Report).

Conveyancing

Once you have the valuation survey secured and cleared as acceptable, you know that the kingpin to the mortgage deal is in place. If you are purchasing with cash then it will be your decision as to whether the survey report is suitable to progress to purchase.

You may have already instructed a solicitor from the start when you agreed on the property purchase. You will have needed the solicitor to be instructed in any case for any mortgage application to be processed as they will need to know who will be legally representing you. The mortgage company will also send a copy of the formal offer of a loan to your solicitor as well as to you.

After a successful valuation, the only thing that I have known which can threaten the deal is something that the conveyancing solicitor may uncover. In that case, it may have been well worth the money you paid to exit the deal, and think yourself lucky you did not get involved.

Assuming all is to go well and to prepare to cover all the up-front payments required for completion, you should ask your solicitor for an estimate of total completion costs to prepare for. Then, just before mortgage completion, you need to request a completion statement. This should show exactly how much you should pay them to complete the purchase.

Insuring

The most basic cover you should have for a property is Buildings Insurance. This will need to be paid in advance of starting the mortgage so this is effectively another up-front cost to consider. It is not strictly just for mortgaging purposes though as you should protect yourself with this even if making a cash purchase of a property.

However, as far as cost considerations go, it is enough to know that this can be covered by payment of a single premium paid in advance for the year, or it can be paid by spreading the payments on say a monthly basis.

The actual cost will depend mainly upon factors such as who you get insured by, the broker you might be using for the insurance, your previous claims history for similar insurance policies, and the exact nature of cover required (for example if the property is ready to let or if some refurbishment is required before first letting).

You are generally free to shop around for your own although some lenders offer their own recommended insurance. Sometimes, if you decide not to take their offer of insurance out, they charge you a small fee for you taking out your own insurance.

This really makes no sense apart from enabling them to make a little more money from you away from the headlines of the deal.

If they do offer you this insurance, they will phone you about it before the mortgage deal completes to get it in place ready for mortgage completion. Sometimes it is just optional and there is no charge to you if you don't take it out from them. I have never taken out the lender's insurance offer, I prefer to use my own insurance broker to do this.

As well as the factors already described, the insurance cost itself is specifically based on the insurance valuation figure that will be determined by the Valuer. The insurers will base their cost for your insurance on a basis of so many pounds annual insurance cost per thousand pounds insured. Don't be tempted into reducing the valuation figure to get a lower quotation as this will possibly invalidate full insurance cover.

In some cases, the insurance value can be much more than the purchase price of the property. This is because the figure includes the full rebuilding of the property to modern building control standards, and will include any necessary demolition costs and site clearance costs.

Important Sidenote:

If you are not mortgaging the property right from the outset as a part of the property purchase, it makes sense to get an independent Registered Institute of Chartered Surveyors (RICS) Valuer in to give you an assessment and a reinstatement value. This reinstatement value for the buildings insurance would be required to be correct if the property was to suffer a major catastrophe and need rebuilding. As the risks are increased during the empty period with refurbishment works, make sure you have the right buildings insurance in place.

Getting the Keys

Getting the keys to a property is the end of one chapter and the start of another in the story of that particular property investment. You have finally done enough to take legal possession and the refurbishment work can start to be planned properly now you know you have the property for sure.

You might well have had some tradesman waiting on stand-by for when you completed on the property, but the first thing will be for you to enter the property and take stock of what you have bought and look for any other details and opportunities you might have overlooked on the property viewing.

In getting the keys, you will first be told by your solicitor that they have made the payment and to contact the agent or seller for the keys. However, the agent or seller will need confirmation from the seller's solicitor that the money has been received and the keys can be released. I find at this stage you will have to do a little chasing to get access to the keys, so be prepared to do just that on completion day.

Congratulations on your investment property purchase!

Step One of BRRRR(R!) completed.

If done correctly, you not only bought an investment property, you bought the right property for your investment strategy.

Refurbish

Financing the Refurbishment Work

The financing of the refurbishment can come from any source of funds that you have access to. This is not like the deposit payment for the mortgage. There will be nobody asking you where you got the money from to do the refurbishment work. The choice is yours and the options are wide and varied. The simplest and probably cheapest is to use any cash you have in the bank. It is not doing much in the bank anyway, so you might as well use it for something productive that will generate an income in the future.

If you don't have access to a bank account with sufficient cash in it, you have many other options, as long as you can handle the credit afforded to you. This can be in terms of family member loans to joint venture agreements, or simply using credit card payments and paying minimum monthly payments until you can get the money back out of the property deal to pay the capital off. This can however prove expensive, depending on the deal you have on the credit card(s) you will be using.

Using credit cards, there is however another way to access cash for very little in interest payment, which you may or may not be aware of. With credit cards, you can raise money short-term by using a credit card that has a *money transfer* capability. This is where the money can be transferred directly into your bank account. This will be paid directly into the same account that you would make the credit card payments from. Not all cards have this ability, although you only need one such card to be able to transfer all your credit card balances into your bank account.

If you have credit cards that do not have this money transfer capability, then you make a *balance transfer* from the card that doesn't to one that does, then transfer the balance from there into your bank account. You can also do this by using up the credit on the money transfer card and then paying it off with a balance transfer from the other card. However, you don't want to use up all lines of credit in case you need to use some more later. In any case, using up all your lines of credit is unwise unless you have absolutely no alternative. If this is the situation, then make this for as short a time as possible as you don't want to continually operate in property investment, being in this financial position.

You could use credit cards to finance such things as the materials for the refurbishment work as well and this would not even require a balance transfer. However, make sure any credit card purchasing is not on a high rate. Money transfers and balance transfers are generally much cheaper than paying the interest rate on card purchases, so transfer the balance or pay the balance off in full when payment is due.

Furthermore, some credit cards even offer zero percent on purchases for a while after first acquiring the card. In this case, it is sensible to keep the balance while it is zero percent and pay it off just before it goes to the higher rate. You do this by just paying the minimum monthly amount and can set up automatic payment for this with the credit card company, this will also avoid any missed payments and the consequences that these could have on your credit rating.

Credit card money does have to be managed carefully and you should take some advice on this. In general, though, the things to watch out for are ensuring that you only use this as short-term finance and that you don't find yourself being forced on to a high rate of interest. Anything above what you would normally pay for a mortgage is high as far as I am concerned. The transfers you are taking out should also ideally be zero percent transfer deals for nearly a year or more and with a low transfer fee such as no higher than 3%.

You should also be looking at having it for at least nine months before it reverts to the high rate of interest, although a much longer time would be better. You have to be comfortable that you can handle credit well for this, don't move into this area of borrowing lightly. I have personally had over £60,000 on credit cards at the same time, this was taken as cash to use out of a total line of credit (all my card lending limits added up) of £80,000. These days my balance is much lower, although for a short period I was managing things this way to help finance refurbishment projects, then refinancing to pay it off as part of the BRRRR process.

Personal loans are another thing you can use to raise a cash balance. Although sometimes you will be asked what the reason for the loan is, then it is up to the lender whether they make you the loan or not. However, property upgrade work is often seen as a safe thing to do with the money, often termed *home improvements*. Therefore, you could always let them know that you are to use it for a property refurbishment project.

However, be aware that the overall balance of any debts you are paying off will also have a bearing on the decision to lend when it comes to the remortgage which releases the capital tied up in the property under refurbishment. This will represent what the lender sees as your financial stability or instability. They don't want to see that you are overexposed on any lines of borrowing, including credit card balances or any other unsecured loans in particular.

In fact, for such unsecured debt as credit card debt, they will look at what you are currently borrowing as a proportion of the borrowing limit on your portfolio of credit cards, especially if it is a high amount in say the tens of thousands you are owing. Take advice from your mortgage broker as to what is likely to be an acceptable maximum you can extract using this approach, in order not to threaten the likelihood of getting the refinance approved.

A loan from a family member is a common thing in property investment, where there is support for this from other members of the family that is. Whilst this is not something that is allowed for raising money for a deposit payment for a mortgage, it is fine to do it for refurbishment work. You can formalise the loan agreement from the family member by using a solicitor or however you like depending on your relationship with them.

You can also agree whatever you want regarding the rewards to them as long as you both agree; this might include payment at the end, where you return the money to them after remortgaging the property, or by monthly interest payments. Or any combination in whatever proportions are agreeable. The best thing is to keep it as simple as possible to reduce the chances of misunderstandings arising.

Hopefully, you have access to the money for the refurbishment work without going to these extents, but the options are there for you should you need them, especially in your early days of starting out with BRRRR.

Light Refurbishment

The level of refurbishment for BRRRR projects was already discussed in brief in the previous chapter on buying. This is because you need to spot the opportunity for adding value at that stage, and that comes from refurbishment programmes. Included in the general term of refurbishment in BRRRR is property remodelling. If we were to go to a more major extent of changes in the property that would be considered as development work. With BRRRR we are certainly not looking to become a developer.

What we are doing is trying to hit the sweet spot of adding the absolute highest value but for the minimum amount of work. At the same time, we are looking to use the work as a lever to raise the value as much as possible. This has been covered previously in the section on adding value. There is therefore a bias towards keeping the refurbishment as light as possible but whilst increasing value sufficiently to get the valuation we require on refinancing. This will be a property valuation sufficient to extract our invested capital, which includes both our deposit money and refurbishment money.

The term light refurbishment will also appear in some mortgage products that allow for a certain level of improvement, as already discussed under the section on refurbishment mortgages. However, any mortgage that is offered will also take into account the state of the property at purchase and will also be looking to ensure the level of works is not too major. The term *light refurbishment* may come up again in such lending considerations, and this will be a judgement call by the Valuer as to whether a mortgage deal should be offered at all.

When you get into deeper refurbishment and remodelling work, you will often be looking to use a bridging loan. These are more expensive finance products and expect a larger amount of deposit to be offered in order to manage the additional risk associated with such lending. That means you can still take on these projects if the numbers stack up and you will be using the same BRRRR principles. Certainly, when you are starting out, you should be looking at the lighter end of refurbishment work.

You may well be starting to think about what exactly constitutes light refurbishment work. The previously discussed adding of bedrooms by simply subdivision of existing and the formation of ensuites in existing bedrooms, as well as the addition of a bathroom or toilet can be considered at the deeper end of what constitutes light refurbishment, and also termed *property remodelling*. We will now look at some examples of typical light refurbishments.

What would be absolutely acceptable in the classification of light refurbishment is the straight replacement of kitchen units and replacement of bathroom suites. Replacing a heating system that is beyond current standards with old radiators and an old boiler would normally be seen as an absolute must under a light refurbishment programme. Changing the windows and external doors would still be considered as part of a light refurbishment programme, which would also be seen as a must if you are looking to get maximum value and these elements of the property are crying out for attention.

On top of this, there would be the almost obligatory full redecoration of the property and replacement of any worn floor coverings. We have also already mentioned improving the condition of the walls and ceilings, especially where there is old Artex that needs covering up or removing.

I think you will be able to see already that these works alone can start leaning heavily on the refurbishment budget. You will therefore need to make some assessments as to how you can do the facelift work most cost-effectively, and start to consider things such as just changing the doors on the existing kitchen units rather than replace the whole lot.

This will be only possible if the kitchen unit carcasses are in good condition, and you will need to assess that in detail to avoid false economy and having to revisit this area again later. Expertly painting over existing units can also work, as long as doors are in good physical condition, in addition to the carcasses.

Partially changing out the bathroom suite would be another option to consider if some parts looked more in need than others, to help manage the budget. Maybe just changing the taps and adding a shower with a shower screen would be an option in some situations to transform the way the bathroom looks. Perhaps also replacing or adding some tiling, but avoiding fully fitting out with tiles would be another.

You should now be able to see how you will need to develop some experience with this element of BRRRR. This experience and expertise are all about finding where the most value is to be added for the minimum of cost. The difference between the cost and the value added is going to be the real uplift in value that you can extract from the refinancing exercise.

Property Remodelling and Developing

If we consider remodelling of a property a kind of halfway house between a refurbishment programme and property developing, we won't be far off a good definition of it. Sometimes the work on a BRRRR project touches on remodelling by adding rooms as already discussed, but it stops short of developing in the sense that there is no heavy building work taking place.

Developing would include things like removing structural walls and using part of the outside space to build an extension to the property. These are definitely not the areas that we should be looking at for improvement works when using BRRRR. You can consider these as property developer activities. That is not to say that you can't still apply the BRRRR principles to recycle money, but in these steps, you are more likely looking to sell the property to release the money rather than refinance it.

The reason for having to sell when property developing, in most cases, is that the value of the property is raised beyond an amount of a loan from which the interest payments could be supported by the rental income. In other words, the deal does not stack up for a refinance. BRRRR is about investment property portfolio building and then holding the property portfolio for a long time, during which there should be a natural increase in property values for your wealth to benefit from.

Property Conversions

A property conversion in the sense of converting it from one use to another can also come into the BRRRR equation. This would then be part of the strategy that you look for when implementing this approach. Ideally, it would fall within the definitions more akin to the heavier end of a light refurbishment programme with most probably an element of property remodelling. Because of this, the approach for property use conversion with BRRRR has more often been to convert a house (use class C3) to a house in multiple occupation (use class C4).

Where there is no Article 4 planning restrictions in place in the locality of the property, C3 to C4 conversion can be allowed as permitted development and no planning application is required. These also work for BRRRR because although there are considerable additional costs to make the conversion, the uplift in rental income potential has moved from single let to multi-let, usually quadrupling the rental income or thereabouts.

We should not get too excited about this however as there will normally be liabilities to cover such as council tax, utilities, and WiFi. Nonetheless, the mortgage that can be taken out of the property can be significantly higher if you can get this on a commercial basis, based on the rental income. This is a model that has worked for some people who have used the BRRRR approach to build up a portfolio of HMOs. I have also used this in building up my HMOs in my overall property portfolio, meaning my HMOs are fully financed with loaned money and none of my money left in.

We currently have the permitted development right opportunity for commercial to residential property conversions. These can also work using the BRRRR model, albeit including an element of remodelling and bordering on property development maybe. It will all depend on the layout of the commercial property that you are taking on to convert to residential (either single let units, or HMO rooms). The big opportunity comes from the fact that commercial property tends to be cheaper per square metre than residential property.

When you then make the use conversion from commercial to residential, you naturally assume that uplift in value as you take it from one use form to the other. There is of course considerable work input required to make the conversion happen, but the uplift in value will be commensurate and the sums can still add up. We are now at the more adventurous end of BRRRR here, and not the staple end which is the light refurbishment and renting out of properties that are then refinanced for a higher loan amount to release your invested capital. But the principles remain the same.

One caveat to mention regarding the aforementioned residential conversion to HMO, is that if you are buying with a mortgage you need to be careful. This is because I am not aware of any current mortgage products that allow for a property conversion like this. If you took out a standard single let mortgage for the purchase, you do not have the lender's permission to carry out the HMO conversion work. The other twist is that you cannot get an HMO mortgage because when you purchase it then it is not classed as an HMO (even if your intention is to convert during an otherwise light refurbishment project).

The solution to this scenario is to either buy with cash or to use a bridging loan and then refinance onto an HMO mortgage when it is ready and has all the certifications in place that are required for its operation.

Obtaining Permissions

You will need to be aware of what permissions you need to carry out the work plan. In most cases, this will include the involvement of the local council. There are two key departments at the council that you will need to work with, these are the Planning Department and the Building Control Department. Depending on the intentions for your work you might also need to involve the Housing Standards Regulatory Control department, who tend to get involved in HMO development work and give out any required licensing.

For most of the refurbishment work, it will simply come under the Building Control Department. This department needs to be informed whenever you have any remodelling work involved. This can be done either by submitting a Building Notice to the council or by doing what is known as a Full Plans Application. For the smaller work you will be doing in BRRRR then a Building Notice should be sufficient. I have taken both approaches, with the full plans approach being used for converting houses to HMOs.

The building notice will not require any plans to be drawn up, instead, you will need to simply give a short description of what you are going to be doing. A building control inspector will then make contact with you and come out to look at the work proposal on-site with you. In my experience, the building control inspectors have been very helpful in commenting on the work and pointing out what needs to be done to have it done correctly.

The building control inspector will then periodically return to check on the progress of the work. You can call them to take a look at key stages where they can see what is being done and to ensure they are happy with it. They might agree to accept photos of some work that will be covered up by plastering if they can't attend in time. Otherwise, you will have to work with them and try to schedule the work and their inspection visits accordingly.

For the smaller jobs, they will not be too bothered about closely monitoring the work, but there will need to be a call out to them when the work is complete to get the building notice signed off. This will be to state that the work was done in accordance with building regulations and a copy will be held on their files and available by public search. This then forms a record of changes that were made at a property and confirms conformance to the building regulations.

A similar approach is taken for a full plans application and they will need a visit to the site, as well to approve the start of the work. You should not start any work until they have given permission, although I have found that, in practice, they are quite flexible on this. However, they need to come to make any appropriate observations or suggestions so a visit from them as soon as possible around the start date of the work will be required. This will also depend on the speed of the work's progress, therefore it is better to comply and get them out before the work starts if you possibly can.

There are individual standards in building regulations required for any plumbing, heating, electrical installation, and double-glazing installations or alterations. These can normally most easily be complied with simply by the work of a trained tradesman in each area. They essentially self-certify the work as compliance with building regulation standards. With the exception of the plumbing work, you should get conformance certificates issued which are all managed by the tradesmen and you should receive copies in the post later.

If the above work forms part of the building control application, made either by a building notice or a full plans application, the building control inspector will request copies of the certifications before signing off a project as completed and compliant.

Obtaining Planning Permission is only necessary when major changes are being made to a property, and, in particular, if it affects the external appearance of a property. You would normally need this for a change of use of a property as well. However, with the recent permitted development rights laws being passed, this has reduced the involvement and influence of the planning department on such matters somewhat. If you are in any doubt about whether what you are doing needs planning permission, simply contact a local planning architect for advice on the matter.

It would be therefore normally expected that for basic BRRRR operations you won't need to involve the planning department. Although it is quite probable that you will need to involve the building control department on some jobs where you are making alterations or remodelling a property. In any case, tradesmens' work should result in the issuing of the relevant installation compliance certificates, so ensure you get these before you pay their invoices.

Refurbishing by Yourself, or by Others?

Unless you are a multi-skilled builder by trade, it is very unlikely you will be doing all the refurbishment work yourself. That said, I think it is a good thing to get involved in some of the early projects if only to get hands-on experience on what is required to do certain jobs. This might fall short of you actually doing skilled jobs such as plastering or jobs that require qualification like electrical work, but anything you can do will help you to appreciate the work that has to go into a project.

Once you have this experience it will help you in deciding whether contractors are giving you reasonable quotes or not for any work you are asking them to do. The other more skilled or qualified work will simply require you to learn by comparing quotations, as well as taking into account the quality of the finished job by each contractor. Maybe you can only work on practical tasks at a basic handyman level, or maybe nothing at all. I found that ripping out and minor demolition tasks were my fortes, not exactly skilled tasks, more like labouring tasks but at least I was getting involved.

No matter what level of practical ability you are at, you will need to learn to manage the various trades and coordinate the work. Unless of course, you get a project manager to do that for you. This would then be another service you will have to pay for and as the margins are tight to make BRRRR work, it is likely you will not be able to afford this luxury. I have known some who do this, but normally the project manager is paid from another source, such as a part of a property agency they are involved with or even own. Clearly, this would come later and not be likely at the start of your property investment ventures using BRRRR.

I think we have therefore already answered the question as to whether to do it yourself or use others. It would be fitting to make another point on this topic which is about the number of working hours that would be needed to do a complete refurbishment. I have never added these hours up, but it is clear to me that it is too much for one person to do this within a reasonable timescale. This is especially if they are also in employment elsewhere and can only work in the evenings and at weekends. I tried my best to do this on my first projects so that I got the experience mentioned before, but the effect was to drag the completion of the project out a long way.

I consider that by completing the work earlier, I reduce the amount of finance charges (assuming I bought with a mortgage) and I get the rental income earlier. I therefore see there is little by way of cost-saving in doing the work myself. On the other hand, you need to be careful about what you pay for others to do the work. That then becomes the challenge to find the right people to do the work for you at reasonable prices.

There is also an argument, that is quite well-known now, which says you should be working *on your business* rather than *in your business.* In the context of BRRRR, that means you should be spending the time looking for the next deal to do rather than working on the property refurbishment job itself. You have much more chance to add value to your business if you take that approach than if you bury your head in the detail of the refurbishment work. Overseeing the work is however another matter, and you should consider that as working on your business, at least when you are starting out in BRRRR you should anyway.

There will be times when it might be best to do the work yourself however, maybe for expediency and assuming you can do the work in the first place. This should be the exception rather than the rule. But don't exempt yourself from doing some work *in your business*, if it makes sense overall.

Assembling your Power Team

The previous discussion brings us naturally onto what is commonly referred to as your *Power Team.* This consists of the business contacts you have to get the work done. Not only included in this are the tradesmen, but also the solicitors and mortgage brokers. Here we focus on the refurbishment side so I will not discuss solicitors and mortgage brokers further, but suffice to say you will need to have good working partners in those professions too. Apply the principles mentioned below to those professions and you will build a well-rounded power team.

Building your power team is about finding the range of tradespeople you need to refurbish and maintain your properties. To start with, you would be best served by asking around for recommendations from people who are already investing in property locally. I have found that often these are not given out freely though, and don't always expect people to give you their best contacts, especially if you don't know them very well. You might well be getting past contacts they have moved on from now, for one reason or another.

The other way is of course to look for the trades in local advertisements in local papers or local online directories or internet searches for local trades. In this way, you will be going in cold with them without recommendations so it really is a gamble. The best way to manage this is to show each person the job you are needing doing and get quotes from them for the work. If you think you are getting a good price from one of them then you can ask to speak to someone that they have done work for in the past and check things out with them directly to make sure that the quality of work is going to be as expected.

The true judgement of the work and price to value will come from when they do the work for you, and that may also impact on your working relationship with them. You will find that you will get on well with some people and not so well with others. How they respond when you change the work specification for some reason will often determine how well you will work with them going forwards. Then you will have to see how they deal with charging you for any extra work you give them that is over and above the original specification. Whether you feel you are getting good value from them will then be up to you to assess.

The other thing you will want to look out for is how punctual they are to attend the work when they say they are going to attend. You will learn that you need certain work doing in a certain order, such as carrying out the electrical work before the finishing-off plastering work, and their punctuality could affect how smoothly the overall job runs.

If you don't manage to get the work done in the right order then it can cause delays and generate extra costs to the project. Lack of punctuality is often an ongoing battle with tradesmen in my experience, some more than others. Follow up with them regularly, don't expect they will do as they say they will, or at least not when they said they will do it.

You will then find that it also helps that the characters of each of your trades get on well with the others. They can decide to work together well or be awkward with each other. This is pretty much a dynamic you cannot be sure about until you get going and get them working together on a project. If you find problems there then you might need to do a little detective work and find out which one might be the main source of problems. That will not be easy to do when you hear different stories coming back from the different people involved in the work.

Maybe you can see already that building your power team will likely be an iterative process and you will need to look out for others who could do the same work. It is good to also have a few people that can do the same work as that keeps everyone on their toes with work prices and quality. When you have just one person for one trade you might well see the pricing rise and work quality decline somewhat. However, dealing with more than one person on different jobs takes more energy than dealing with a main trusted source of that service.

It should be clear to you if you are already interested in property investment, what the main trades are that you will need. But for those who are not so well acquainted yet, I can state the main trades that you will require as being an electrician, a plumber, a heating engineer (oftentimes these also do the plumbing work), a plasterer, a joiner, a builder, a roofer, and a general handyman. You will also need to have trusted suppliers and fitters of floor coverings, although these are needed at the very end of the project when the work is done, so they don't have much interaction with the main core of your power team.

Managing Neighbours
When you have got the keys to the property, it is a good idea to introduce yourself to your new neighbours. Starting out with a good relationship will help the work progress more smoothly. They will also be your eyes and ears for anything that could be a problem while you are not there.

Exchange phone numbers with them if you can so that you can let them know about any works being done that might likely affect them by generating noise or dust for example. You can also expect that they will contact you in case of any problems, but you don't need to mention that when you first meet them and make them think you are putting on them. You don't want to get things off to a bad start, there is plenty of time for things to go wrong in your relationship with them later, just don't bring that on prematurely.

The neighbours will be keen to find out what you are going to be doing with the property. In the case of a refurbishment project, they might be very pleased to hear that if the property looks bad from the outside. Depending if they are an owner-occupier then they might not be so pleased when they find out you are not taking up residence there and that the property will be let out. It is likely however that you will be buying in a rental area where people are well accustomed to short-term rental tenancies.

The thing I have never been able to communicate in a way that leaves the neighbours comfortable, is when I have bought a house to convert to a house in multiple occupation. It is probably right of them to be concerned as these are very challenging properties to manage and there can be more than a fair share of disturbances at times. You will have to try to reassure them that you vet the tenants well and that you will be managing the property well.

There is one legal obligation that you will have to comply with concerning the neighbours, where their house is adjoining to yours. If any work concerns the removal of structural fabric from a wall that adjoins their property, you are required to give them a party wall notice two months before that work commences. This can of course be a problem to the timing of your refurbishment work. However, if you are removing things such as chimney breasts to make more space for a better kitchen fit-out for example, this is something you will need to do if that wall adjoins a neighbouring property.

Other than that, keeping in touch with your neighbours is a matter of it being done in as reasonable a manner as possible to keep goodwill between both of you. You don't want to be dealing with a neighbourly dispute at your new investment property. Although I can't promise you it won't happen. Consider managing neighbours as another skill required for best results with BRRRR.

Ripping Out

The first task on any refurbishment is to remove the contents and building fabric that you intend to remove or replace. Most of this can be done immediately upon acquiring the property. You will most probably need a skip to remove the waste as it can be quite substantial in volume, not to mention the overall weight. If you have a small trailer and tow bracket, you could take some to the municipal domestic waste tip. If it is not too much then you could take it to the waste tip inside a vehicle. However, such waste disposal is not intended for what the council will consider as trade waste. For many reasons, a waste skip is therefore advisable.

Don't be surprised if you soon need to order another skip as they soon fill up. This can often be aided by other people from the locality taking the opportunity of sharing your skip in the evenings. For this reason, it is better to only order the skip for delivery when you are going to be having a hive of activity in filling it, or others may well do it for you, only it will not be filled with your waste!

To reduce the chance of needing to spend money on an additional skip hire I learned to fill it first with the soft furnishings and then put the heavy waste on top as it tends to then compress the volume somewhat. You are only supposed to fill the skips level but you can push it a little and go a little higher. A common trick is to put any waste doors or long boards horizontally along the sides such that these extend up a little to help hold a slight overfilling of the skip. Normally this won't be a problem on collection, as long as it is not unstable at the top and falling off the skip as it is picked up.

If you have any particularly large items that would threaten to ensure that you need a second skip, it could be worth putting those to one side for a while. If these cannot be broken down easily and put in the skip that way, you could contact the council as most offer the service to pick up several large items for a reasonable price. The option of burning household waste to reduce its volume is not allowable any more. Maybe you can get away with something around bonfire night, but you don't want to plan your refurbishments around that single calendar event of course!

Any metal items can be uplifted for free by scrap metal merchants, such as old ovens and washing machines and other similar items can be quite large, it is best to see if these can be taken away for free. If you can put these outside on easy view at the side of the skip, it is likely to disappear by itself in a few days, but it is better to arrange the pick-up to avoid annoying people with the waste items.

Large items that you cannot put in a skip are old fridges and freezers. These will need to be either collected by a council pick-up or by a company that deals with refurbishing such items. The latter may also give you a charge to collect as these are hard items to get rid of since they contain gases that need to be managed.

Once the skip is full, it would be best to contact the skip hire company and request an immediate uplift of it so that it does not get overfilled by people from the neighbourhood. That would mean you have another problem as the skip hire company will not take the skip away because it is overfilled, with other people's waste! There may be a way to deal with that, but better to manage it by getting it taken away straight away than deal with another problem you could have just created by delaying a pick-up.

Planning the Work

You will have had the idea for the refurbishment plan for some time, but the time to get a detailed plan together is when you can call tradesmen from your power team around to the house. Show each workman what you want to do and ideally give them this on a written list they can refer to and add notes to. This will help them when they go away and put a price together for you for the work, and there will be less chance of a misunderstanding regarding what needs to be done.

An important thing to find out from each trade is what work needs to be done first to allow them to do their work. They might need certain things removing to access the parts of the property more easily to do their work. If you can find this out then you can start to plan the order of the work.

Even if you have all the requirements for what needs to be done first before someone can come and do their work, you would also do well to plan the work so that you don't have too many trades working in the property at the same time. There is a tendency for the various trades to get in each other's way it seems, most prefer an empty property to work in, or maybe just one other trade at the same time.

You will soon find this out and find out which trades can work together well enough, but it will depend on the work being carried out at the same time. Maybe each trade can work in a separate area, but it would be no good for them both to work in the kitchen at the same time for example. A work plan that is correctly scheduled and diarised would therefore be ideal, as opposed to just a list of work that needs doing.

Having done all of this, don't expect the work to go to plan like clockwork. Tradesmen have other customers and sometimes emergencies arise. In those cases, they have to attend them just as you would hope they would for you if you were in that situation in the future. The plan will need to flex in accordance with these disruptions but if you have a plan you can work around it more easily than if you just had a worklist to address.

There are times when maybe you have to do some work in the wrong order just to get on with the job. Don't let that stop the work, just be aware that there will be a cost implication. It is better though to keep the job moving even if you have to remove some work that has been done in order to do some other work. Be prepared to get critical comments from the trades when you do things in the wrong order however, but they only see it from their point of view so just shoulder those comments and carry on.

A good example here is one I have already given, as it is a common one, which is the plastering that should wait until any chasing out of existing plaster for electrics and plumbing runs has been done. However, if you are struggling to get some of the trades to do that and the plasterers are available, you might do well to get a day's work done by the plasterers and revisit any subsequent damage to the new plaster later.

Estimating the Costs

A rough estimate of the costs should have been done as part of the decision to buy. In my case, I would get these listed in a spreadsheet to add up the estimated costs for each of the major work items identified. These are based more on experience, or from explaining the job for a rough estimate with a tradesman. On this list, I would also add a contingency figure that would be 15% of the total value of the work estimated. That would be in addition to estimating on the higher side for each item of work.

Using the list that I had prepared for the rough cost estimates used at the property offer stage, I would flesh this out with more detail and a better estimate. This could now more easily be done as I have got full access to the property and can invite the tradesmen to visit and look at the work required.

My objective would be to beat the total figure on the first list by about 20% after all the work had been done. I am then coming out on the safe side of the money expected to have to be put in for the refurbishment work. This makes it more likely that I will get a revaluation figure later that will enable me to pull out my full amount of capital invested. The capital invested includes all money involved in the purchase of the property as well as all other costs up to the date of the remortgage, including all finance and refurbishment related costs.

After a while, you will get a feel for the costs of the work that needs doing, although it could be difficult at the start. It helps in that you are going to be taking on similar properties for refurbishment, therefore the costs estimate for each kind of work item required are likely to be similar. If you were running a business where you were doing properties up to sell, these would likely be more diverse in size and layout, as well as diverse in the kinds of work needing doing. That would make it harder to estimate the costs.

You therefore have the 'copy and paste' advantage in your approach that should help you with these estimating skills quite quickly. This is a good thing because you need to be accurate to make BRRRR work on its naturally repeating cycle.

Controlling Costs

Having got the work plan and the estimate of costs, it is important to track the costs against your budget as you go along. It will be natural that some will go over and some will come in under budget. However, there seems to be a tendency for costs to only increase. This is only natural because you cannot foresee all the details and all the items that need attending to, until you actually start the work.

You should however have estimated on the higher side for each item and that should help include for the work not apparent at the time. If you speak to a tradesman then they might give you a work estimate, just make sure you get a range from them at the time. Use the higher figure for the budget and try to get them to hit the lower figure with the work.

Make this clear to them that you are trying to hit the lower figure and ask if they have any ideas that would help with that. They will know things that are not apparent to you, such as leaving some work items that don't affect the overall outcome of the work. It can be very valuable time if you spend time talking to them about the options. More often than not they will have other work they want to get on to elsewhere so it is in the interests of both parties to find the most efficient way to achieve the end objective.

If you are running well over budget at a certain point, you can either decide to remove another costly item or carry on and take the overspend. If you have to remove a particular item from the worklist, make sure this has the least impact on the end valuation of the property. If you can't find anything to remove to meet this objective, you might do best to stick to the work plan and overspend. At least this will more likely secure your end valuation.

If you cut corners that are visible in your end product after the refurbishment work, you run the risk of getting a lower valuation than you had accounted for. This can then be as bad as overspending as far as recycling your investment cash goes.

Controlling Work Quality

Controlling the quality of the refurbishment work will very much be down to you. A tradesman is generally there to do an acceptable job and get paid for it and then move onto the next job for someone else. They can sometimes cut corners and leave work that they would like others to look after for them, but they still get paid the same amount of money as the work got done. Chief amongst this that is common to nearly all trades, is tidying up after themselves. You should include that they tidy up and remove from the property all the spare materials after their work. Good luck with that one though!

If you don't like the look of something in the work being done, you need to speak up quickly and set the bar for the quality of work that you expect. It might be as well to have a pre-job meeting where you go through the details of what they are intending to do. In particular, this might include where they are going to run wires or pipes for example. You will not want these on show, but they will not be so bothered about that as the work is still installed as per the general request.

It is best to show up and just take a look at the work progressing and see where things are happening that you didn't quite expect. Believe me, you will find something going off the rails, if you repeatedly call in throughout the project activity. It is better to find such things when they are developing rather than when they are fully installed. It is hard to give specific examples as it is often about the details of a particular job. I have already mentioned pipes and wires, and even if they are in surface mounted mini trunking, these can look quite ugly.

Other things might include the finish to a plastering job in terms of how smooth and level it is, straightness of tiling work, how a bath is fitted up against a wall, how secure a toilet feels when it is sat on. On these matters, you should expect that these should be dealt with as standard, but the poor quality of work arising from such lack of attention to detail is quite common and needs to be controlled.

When a workman is challenged by you, they might likely have a reason or excuse for the problem already lined up. No matter what that is you need to use your diplomacy skills to ensure you get what you want. Of course, if it is beyond either the capability or the will of the workman to deliver this, then you need to move on and find someone else to do the work for you.

Finishing Off Work

Irrespective of what I have just said about controlling the quality of the work, there will be items at the end of the work that need closer attention to give better finishing off. These details are matters such as door latches not quite catching, doors sticking when opened or catching on the carpet excessively, paint smudged where it should not be, doors to kitchen units not quite level, door handles sticking etcetera. The list goes on.

These are just little issues that can add up to a bad impression and be annoying for anyone living there in the future, as well as spoiling the cosmetic appearance of the place. It is very important to get these small items attended to as you don't want anything, including the Valuer, to think this is a general sign of the work quality. It won't be of course because you will have been monitoring and controlling that during the project, but they won't be able to appreciate that and can only judge on their experience with these small things.

So common is this phenomenon of the small things accumulating at the end of a project that the process of finding all these details out has been given a colloquial term; that term is 'snagging'. You will therefore need to go through a snagging exercise at the end of a project, and also after each tradesman is asking to be paid as far as the work they have done so far goes.

It is common for larger building contracts to have a retention amount of about 5% that is only released after all the snagging works have been done to satisfaction. If attention to details was there in the first place, you would not need to do this, however, it is such that this snagging exercise has to be part of the process. In some cases, you might be as well to have a handyman come with you to do all the small items, where a general handyman can do such work, as is normally the case on finishing off items.

Certifications

Certifications are the certificates that you should collect for your project file as you go along. We have already mentioned what most of these are in the section on permissions, but it is worth stating again that you should collect these and file them together with any other important property information.

These may be requested by the conveyancing solicitor if you eventually sell the property, as most certainly the buyer's solicitor will want to see these. Some of the certifications, like the certificate of building regulations compliance, will be available for access electronically, but you might need to keep paper copies of the other certificates to hand. You might also need to provide these for a refinance and therefore it is essential to treat this matter seriously.

It is easy to overlook the collection and collation of the relevant certifications, but if you don't then this could come back on you later and create more work in getting copies at a later date.

Congratulations on your investment property refurbishment!

Step Two of BRRRR(R!) completed.

If done correctly, you not only refurbished an investment property, you did it to the required specification, completed the work within budget and to the required quality level; with all the work certifications held on file for future reference.

Refinance

Understanding Mortgage Finance

I have already covered the details of UK mortgage finance in depth in my book *All About Buy to Let Mortgages*. That book covers all the essentials that you need to know to avoid all the major mistakes and misunderstandings when dealing with both mortgage and remortgage finance.

I will now cover in this chapter some of the main points that you need to know regarding using mortgages for refinancing to release your capital, but the finer points of this area will be well worth your further study from my other book on the specific topic.

At the time of writing, the UK buy-to-let mortgage market is currently still consumer unregulated so there is nobody to turn to if it all goes wrong. This is unlike the UK residential mortgage market where you can complain to the Financial Ombudsman if you believe you have a case for being treated unfairly or have been misled.

This is now starting to change with a focus on what is being termed the Consumer buy-to-let market. However, this is more for unintentional novice landlords being forced into letting out a property, typically because they cannot sell it at the price they need to sell at due to market conditions for example.

I have never had any reason for appealing to anyone for a poor deal though, if it's a poor deal then I can always remortgage away from it. Probably at a cost of course, but in the scheme of investing figures, this will not be overly significant. Having said that, this is another reason that you must educate yourself in this area of buy-to-let mortgages as it really is a case of buyer beware.

Even if you are taking what is often still termed as professional advice in this area, such as from an Independent Financial Advisor (IFA) or Mortgage Broker, you are still in the same situation with no regulatory body to appeal to if you consider matters have been dealt with unfairly.

Also, be aware that the whole matter of buy-to-let and its related mortgage products can be a fast-changing area; take this book as a general guide and seek specific up to date information at the time of seeking finance. Make sure this is also the latest edition of this book that you can get, especially if you are quite unfamiliar with the current mortgage marketplace.

The term *mortgage product*, by the way, is often simply abbreviated to just *product* by mortgage professionals when discussing mortgage deals. You will get used to that kind of abbreviated terminology and you just need to add it to your vocabulary of mortgaging jargon.

As regards the Mortgagee and Mortgagor relationship, this may be contrary to what you expect. Legally speaking, you offer the lender a mortgage on the property so the lender is termed the mortgagee and you are termed the mortgagor. The mortgagee (the lender) then gives you a loan of the money covered by the mortgage document you sign as the mortgagor; this creates a lien on the title of the property in favour of the lender. This is then their security for the loan of money made to you, which they require you to pay back at the latest by a specific date as stated in the mortgage agreement.

To get a mortgage, you are giving the lender the right to repossess your property and sell it if you don't keep up your mortgage payments. Further, if the price they get for the property sale does not clear the loan and any associated costs accrued, they then have the right to pursue you for the balance through general debt recovery procedures available in UK law. Therefore, the lender has you in a position where you simply can't just walk away from your monthly mortgage payment obligations without serious consequences.

Remortgaging

As we have covered already, remortgaging is basically exchanging the loan capital in one mortgage for a different mortgage. This is usually about switching to a different mortgage with more favourable terms and conditions, and/or for a different amount of capital. As you now should know, the same terminology of remortgaging is used for taking a mortgage out on a property that you may already own outright without any loan first charges attached.

Because remortgaging allows for a change from your present mortgage product to another mortgage product, either with the same or different lender, this gives you full flexibility in choosing the best mortgage deals available on the market at any given time.

Remortgaging also allows you to release a proportion of any increase in the market value of your property as cash into your bank account without having to sell the property. It is this feature that has allowed many ordinary people with modest amounts of starting capital at their disposal to build property portfolios worth many millions of pounds using BRRRR. In these cases, this has often been done in the space of a few years, or even less where they have wanted to do it so quickly. It is the remortgaging and releasing of equity option that has allowed this to happen for them.

Not all countries in the world allow for the same model of remortgaging as we presently have in the UK. For example, some other countries will not allow equity release or even take rental income into account when determining the affordability of a loan for a second property. It is not possible to know how long ordinary people in the UK will continue to have access to buy-to-let remortgaging in the present easily accessible form that we have here in the UK today.

Even recently, legislation and guidance on mortgage lending have brought in restrictions and prohibitions on remortgaging practices commonly used by property investors in the past. Most notably is the introduction of the six-month rule which means you need to have owned the property for six months before being able to apply for a remortgage, even if you bought it for cash.

However, for the time being, we still have the possibility to quickly expand our property portfolios using remortgaging, especially when used with the BRRRR approach. It is best to take advantage of this opportunity while it is here.

Of course, if remortgaging is used incorrectly it can also be dangerous. This is because it can quickly expose people to financial obligations to pay significant mortgage payments each month. Investment in the right properties is essential and so is not remortgaging above an amount for what you will be able to generate the rental income sufficient to pay at least the interest on.

It is to your benefit to ensure that you can easily afford the interest payments from the rental income. You should assess the rental income potential in more detail rather than rely on a lender's simple interest cover ratio that they use. If you got this seriously wrong it could even lead to bankruptcy in extreme cases; take this aspect very seriously.

However, used correctly, and with the purchase of the right kinds of rental properties, then remortgaging can be a very powerful way to build up a high-value property portfolio in a very short time period. This will be so much faster than would be possible for most people simply saving for a deposit before buying each investment property. In comparison to this approach of save-to-invest, rapid remortgaging with equity-release basically turbo-charges property investment for anyone able to use it correctly with the BRRRR approach.

Alternative Refinancing Methods
There are alternative refinancing methods to using a remortgage, but in most cases, a remortgage will be the cheapest and best way for BRRRR.

You could take on private finance by Joint Venture partners, to generate the money to pay off any mortgage finance agreement as well as putting all the original investment money back in your pocket. This would likely mean paying the private finance investors an agreed interest rate or even offering them a part of the equity in the property.

This is messy to achieve and is almost always going to be giving more away than if you did a conventional remortgage. Private finance is however another tool for some investors who are happy to work this way, but it has to be where you have high rental returns from your property to pay the higher monthly payments that are more likely to be associated with this approach.

Another way to use bank finance in the case that you bought the property with a mortgage, is to ask for a *further advance* from the lender. They might offer this at the same interest rate as the original loan or at a slightly different rate to reflect the increased risk they perceive is being taken. It will however require a revaluation although there will be no conveyancing involved. I have used this approach on a few properties and I have two separate mortgages registered against those properties, both by the same lender of course and both first charge mortgages.

The difficulty with this approach for BRRRR is that you are using the same lender and it will likely also be the original Valuer that comes out to do the revaluation. In this situation, it will take a lot of persuading to get the Valuer to value up the property based on the changes you have made in order to get sufficient uplift in value to get BRRRR to work and release all your invested capital. You could try this though, as it will only cost you the price of the revaluation if it does not work for you based on the revaluation figure achieved.

Overall, the remortgage approach is most likely going to be the best way to get what you want from BRRRR and probably remortgaging using a different lender, if you used a lender to finance the purchase that is.

Remortgaging to the Best Deals

Finding the best deals for you is the service the mortgage brokers are supposed to be able to offer you. However, they don't know what the future holds and neither do you. They can only offer what they think is best for you at the time. Changes in wholesale interest rates could affect the effectiveness of this decision in future. It helps if you can at least understand *why* they are proposing a particular product and maybe have you own opinion to challenge them on. At the end of the day, this is about your money, so you should show a strong interest and challenge anything you have questions about.

If you are going to stay in property investment for quite some time, which is the intention of buy-to-let investing, then it is likely that you will look back and wish you had chosen a different mortgage product for some of your properties. If you took your best decision at the time then there is nothing you could have done about this so you will just have to let those feelings go. We don't have crystal balls to use when taking such decisions, we just have an idea of what we think might happen in the future and we have to use that instead.

I have taken some decisions, where it was going to save me a few thousands of pounds on up-front fees, only to find out later that I have lost many thousands against what I could have had if I had selected a different mortgage. Remember mortgages are for a long time so it is easy to make decisions that can gain or lose you many thousands of pounds over the long term.

My regret was not taking out some small margin above base-rate tracking products (explained later) even though there were some very significant up-front fees. With hindsight, I should have taken these deals as the base rate went so low that for those mortgages I would be paying hardly anything right now. However, not many people predicted base rates coming crashing down, not even the banks that were lending with life-of-loan base rate trackers.

Therefore, be mentally prepared to be wrong in your decisions over the longer term, while trying to make your best decisions all the time. Just remember that you don't have a crystal ball, the future can work in your favour as well as against you. Be prepared to take the rough with the smooth. In the end, it should hopefully even out, as long as you take what seem to be the best decisions at the time with the information available.

To be able to take the basic financial decisions needed for a remortgage product, it will be necessary for you to be conversant with the basic interest rate terms that a mortgage may be offered to you on. I have covered these in detail in my book *All About Buy to Let Mortgages* in Chapter Six. However, for convenience and to check your knowledge on these, I have reproduced the summary sections on each main format of interest rate offerings below.

If you don't understand some of the terms or abbreviations mentioned below, you would do well to do a little further study on this topic.

Fixed Rate Mortgages

PROS:

- These mortgages can be the cheapest type of mortgage to take out when interest rates are generally increasing over time.
- There is certainty in taking out these mortgages as the interest rate chargeable stays the same even if interest rates are generally rising.

CONS:

- The longer the period you fix for then typically the higher the fixed interest rate and/or higher the mortgage arrangement fees will be.
- If interest rates were to drop in general, then you will be typically paying more for your mortgage payments during that time of lower general interest rates.
- You will probably pay a significant arrangement fee to get a deal that is fixed for a defined period.
- If you want to exit the deal because rates have fallen significantly then there will likely be a significant early repayment charge (ERC) for doing this during the fixed period.
- The interest rate will suddenly change at the end of the fixed period and likely to revert to Standard Variable Rate (SVR) or a tracker rate that could be higher than the fixed rate.

Variable Rate Mortgages

PROS:

- These mortgages can be the cheapest type of mortgage to take out when interest rates are generally reducing or staying low over time.
- The interest rate chargeable reduces when there is a general reduction in interest rates (the specifics of this depends on the particular type of variable rate mortgage deal).

CONS:

- There is uncertainty in taking out these mortgages because rates might increase leading to affordability issues (depending on the level of increase).
- The interest rate chargeable increases when there is a general increase in interest rates (the specifics of this depends on the particular type of variable rate mortgage deal).
- The kind of variable rate deal available can vary significantly leading to more decision-making to get the likely best deal.

Standard Variable Rate (SVR) Mortgages

PROS:

- These mortgages can be the cheapest type of mortgage to take out as far as mortgage arrangement fees go.
- SVR can be reasonably competitive with other rates if you find a good deal.
- There is no sudden change in rate applied at some point in the near future, as there is no introductory rate offer period applied.

CONS:

- The rate is significantly higher than the rates offered on another basis within an initial offer period.
- The SVR rate can vary significantly from one lender to another.
- The SVR rate can be altered by the lender at any time they see fit.
- If the Bank Base Rate (BBR) is reduced then this does not mean that the lender will do the same, and if they do it can be at some time in the future rather than immediately.
- If the BBR is increased then it is likely that the lender will see this as a reason to increase their rates by the same amount and they will likely do this straight away.

Discounted Standard Variable Rate Mortgages

PROS:

- The rate during the introductory offer period can be very low compared to prevailing interest rates being charged.
- You can secure this situation for a fixed length of time to get significantly cheaper mortgage payments.

CONS:

- These mortgages can be quite expensive to take out as far as mortgage arrangement fees go, although these can be added to the loan.
- The SVR rate can vary significantly from one lender to another so you need to look at the charged rate after discount to compare.
- The SVR rate can be altered by the lender at any time they see fit, for reasons of their own, and this will affect your discounted product by the same amount.
- If the BBR is reduced then this does not mean that the lender will do the same, and if they do it can be at some time in the future rather than immediately.
- If the BBR is increased then it is likely that the lender will see this as a reason to increase their rates by the same amount and they will likely do this straight away.

Going Direct to Lender

You won't get any independent mortgage selection or investment advice by going direct to lenders, whether it be one from a high street bank or one of the specialist buy-to-let lenders. They will simply just give you details on how their specific products work. Although they can offer some good deals, if you feel confident you can select your own remortgage to suit your particular requirements.

You can find deals direct from lenders on the lenders' internet websites, as well as on mortgage product comparison websites. It is worth looking at because the direct-to-lender deals may represent the current best deals available online. However, there might be better deals available only through financial advisors or mortgage brokers; some specialist lenders don't deal directly with the public as they are not set up to manage their business this way.

This is not a problem for the specialist lenders as most daily business with mortgages in the marketplace is done through mortgage brokers; they are only missing the smallest part of the market by operating this way. They can reduce their overheads in operating this way and keep their deals as competitive as possible. It is typical for new lenders and smaller lenders to take this route and put their offerings to the market through mortgage brokers.

Even if you plan to go direct to a lender, it is always good to ask a mortgage broker what deals they can find which might beat what you have found. If you do this, then don't tell the intermediary the specifics of any good deals you have located already, just in case this could influence their response.

Some mortgage brokers or advisors, especially the larger ones, can have access to slightly cheaper rates than the lenders are advertising, as well as special deals such as valuation fee refunds and free legal fees for example. These advantages alone might make it a better deal than going direct to the lender. Therefore, do make a final check before you press the button to commit to going direct to a lender.

You can also ask your broker or advisor to do a search on direct-to-lender deals for you as well and give you the results of their work. I have always found a very honest approach is taken when such a request is made for them to search direct-to-lender deals. Maybe this is because I have a good relationship with my broker. Although be aware that you also can do this yourself, in case you don't have that trusting relationship yet. Although, as already stated, the best buy-to-let deals are likely to be the ones available through mortgage brokers.

As you get more experienced in dealing with mortgages and mortgage brokers, you should start to fully understand what you are doing so you can be in a position to more confidently go direct to lenders and choose your own mortgages in future if you want to. This will become especially valuable if you have developed a focus on a particular property niche, where you need to find the best mortgage products to finance that area of property investment.

Choosing a Mortgage Broker

Both Mortgage Brokers and Independent Financial Advisors (IFAs) act as so-called *intermediaries* in that they are separate from the financial operators who lend the money, but rather they service them by processing their loan applications. As the name implies, intermediaries sit between you and the lender. Be aware though that some intermediaries are not specialists in dealing with buy-to-let mortgages so it is best to find an intermediary that is. Just because they can get you a buy-to-let mortgage does not mean they are specialists in that area.

With mortgages, there are also the two basic areas of specialism which are Residential and Buy-to-let Mortgages. These are the two basic categories of mortgages and you at least must make sure the intermediary you select is experienced in the particular area you want. If the mortgage is for your own home then you need a residential mortgage specialist, and if it is for buy-to-let then you need a specialist in buy-to-let mortgages. Of course, some can deal in both and that is fine as long as they are specialists in each area as opposed to just being able to provide you with a mortgage.

Additionally, make sure they specialise in your particular area of specific mortgage requirement as closely as possible. In other words, they have done deals for similar properties for similar rental purposes in the recent past. Sometimes this is not possible if you are looking for a very special niche-lending requirement. However, in most cases, they should have dealt with the broader category of what you are looking to borrow the money for. You can only find this out by discussing the details with them and gauging their responses.

In addition to the mortgage broker or advisor being a specialist in buy-to-let mortgage lending, it is also preferable that they are familiar with buy-to-let investing strategies; this is so they can help advise you on what you want to achieve. When you are first starting out investing, maybe this is not that important as you will not be looking at advanced approaches to borrowing and using the more creative strategies. However, you should be looking to detect how well they can understand what you want and offer lending solutions to the more difficult projects so that you can be comfortable they will add significant value in your business relationship.

You might find such knowledgeable intermediaries through networking with other property investors or at property events and meetings, or in the media. However, make sure you satisfy yourself that they can help you specifically in the area of property investing you are working in, or look for another.

Intermediaries assist in giving you options or advice on suitable choices that are available in the market and then assisting with processing the application for the chosen mortgage deal. The intermediaries take a commission from the lender as well as likely charging you a fee also. They should, however, have a good working knowledge of all the mortgage products available and be of special value to anyone with an unusual personal situation, or wanting to get a loan for a fairly unusual property or a difficult personal situation. They are of course very valuable to someone simply new to buy-to-let mortgages, to help guide them through the mortgage selection and application process.

However, absolutely make sure you use a *whole of market* mortgage broker who has access to every deal available and specifically ask for this. Being *whole of the market* means they are truly able to be independent in giving you advice for your situation on which is the best product currently available in the whole of the market.

Be wary of some brokers that may seem to be advising widely although, in fact, they are so-called *Tied Brokers* in that they are restricted to a limited panel of lenders. Whole-of-market intermediaries use special search tools like Trigold Prospector and Mortgage Brain that searches all UK mortgages available on the market. These search tools are only available to professional intermediaries. If it is a larger intermediary company you are dealing with, they might have their own even more sophisticated version of these mortgage search systems.

These search tools, together with the trained and experienced advisors, should help find you the best deals available for your particular lending requirement. Finding the right company to help you is the trick as far as you are concerned. Then after that, you can rely on their professional abilities together with you asking them the right questions. The knowledge given should have adequately equipped you in this respect.

When you use a mortgage broker or financial advisor, be sure to ask specifically why they recommend a particular product or selection of products to you. You can then understand how well they are matching your requirements to the products and learn from this for the future. This will help you in your learning experience and can assist you in future decision-making as well as making the right decision for the present deals you are looking at.

The Valuation

The market value of a property for a remortgage will be established by the lender's Valuer who will base this on a range of actual sold prices of comparable properties (often shortened to simply comparables or even comps). Comparables are similar properties accounting for the size, location, type and condition of the property.

All this information is available to a Valuer online apart from, of course, the condition of the property; this aspect of the property condition in particular gives some degree of variation in the final valuation. In this way, although based on certain available facts, the valuation assessment is more of an art rather than an exact science and influenced significantly by the state of repair of the property (hence the need for attention to detail after refurbishment as a part of the BRRRR process).

It is required however that you state on your remortgage application what you think the property is worth; the valuer's job is then basically to either agree with this or provide a different valuation. Typically, any difference to your valuation figure is more often lower than you stated, but it can be higher. You then will be offered the remortgage based on the value that the valuer has assigned to the property. For this reason, it is best to go in with your property valuation figure on the high side rather than the low side, although it should also still be realistic and justifiable.

If you go in too low it is likely that, where the valuer is of a conservative nature, they will simply agree with you even though they might have otherwise valued it higher. If you go in with slightly too high a valuation figure, they then will simply assign what they actually think the property is worth, or they might even agree with you. In this way, you will at least get the highest possible valuation from the valuer. You will have worked out before even investing in the property as to what the value should be when refurbished, so you at least need to target that as the valuation figure.

After some time of investing in a specific area, you will get a good feel for what a property should value up at. This is because you will have had a lot of experience in going to view properties and comparing against what the asking prices are. You should also account for the fact that sale prices will typically be somewhat lower than the asking prices, although sale prices could also be higher than asking prices depending on the specific area. Sold prices will eventually appear online on the various websites including that of the Land Registry of course. This is all what should be accounted for back at the first step of buying a property in BRRRR.

Assuming you have a mortgage on the property already from purchase, remortgaging soon afterwards with a different lender to the one you are with may well get you a more realistic valuation than staying with the same lender. If you remortgage with the existing lender they will have access to the details of some or all of the lending history and might feel your increase in valuation is not justifiable based on that information. However, with a new lender, they will have no such information to consult and will therefore more likely make a valuation based on the true comparable information alone to establish a market value for the property.

After paying for the valuation, you will need to supply some contact details for access to the property and this should be you or someone else you work with and trust who

102

attends that valuation. Probably during the next few days after paying, you will be contacted to arrange the date and time of the valuation.

When the surveyor arrives at the property, notes will be taken on its construction and condition and some key measurements made. This normally does not take very long as it is not an in-depth survey, just a valuation for the purpose of mortgaging. Some of the work will already have been done or will be done later, by using online information to help assess the property value and rental value.

The Valuation Report mostly consists of an account of a physical survey of the property. This is looking for any obvious major problems that could adversely affect the value of the property, as well as the general condition of the property. It will describe such things as the basic construction of the property, the approximate size of the property, the number and type of rooms, any built-in facilities that characterise the house and approximate age of construction.

The most important results are of course the property valuation figure and the rental income assessment.

The Valuer
The Valuer is assigned by lenders from what they call their *Panel of Surveyors.* This means a selection of valuation companies they use and have faith in to provide them with the right level of diligence in valuation that they require. The largest nationwide valuation companies often used by UK buy-to-let lenders as part of their panel of lenders are Connells, Allied, Colleys and Eserve.

However, these companies may also have sub-panels of valuation companies that they send out to you so you never can be sure who exactly will be doing the valuation. The most predictable ones, where you could see the same Valuer many times, are the lender's in-house valuers. These people are dedicated to a specific geographical area and they work for the lender directly rather than being from a separate surveying company on the lender's panel.

In this case, you will often meet the same surveyor when you apply for further remortgages with the same lender. This can be an advantage as they can get to know and trust you more, especially if you are open and honest with them and don't push them too far by trying to get any unreasonable valuations through.

The lenders' valuers, whether in-house or from a panel, will be likely to value more pessimistically than an independent surveyor, who you might have sought some advice from independently regarding property valuations. Therefore, you need to do all you can to give them evidence to support the valuation. Note that the Valuer is key to getting the valuation you require as there is often much at their discretion and a good valuation is often essential in getting the loan amount you want for the BRRRR formula to work.

Wherever possible, meet the Valuer and build a professional relationship with them. This is especially so if you are building a mortgage portfolio with the same lender and possibly the very same Valuer coming out to see you each time. Answer their questions confidently and positively, think beforehand about what they might ask you and be clear on your answers. Even do some work on the internet and provide some documentation showing similar property sold prices that could also be considered as true comparables from the same locality.

Panel Valuers don't get paid anywhere near what you are being charged for the survey, therefore they often won't want to take too long over the valuation. Any work you can help them with like the comparables of value and rental incomes could be gratefully received. It is then their decision if they use it or do further separate research. If they don't have the time they might well just go ahead and use what you have supplied if they feel it seems reasonable.

Meeting the Valuer at the property is very important for remortgaging, as they will have questions as to why you might be claiming the value has gone up since you first bought it. You need to answer these questions, whether they ask these questions or not, by providing them with the information to support this. If you don't do this then you might as well not be at the remortgage valuation, to be honest. You are there to influence the outcome in the best possible way as it is in your interests to do that, at least in a subtle and helpful way.

It could be as simple as a list of improvements made, and if so then provide this on paper for them to take away. You could further also include some proof of costs, such as copies of invoices if this helps your case. If you have a copy of floor plans done to scale then this will be appreciated as they won't have to spend time measuring up the whole building. This can only help your relationship with them of course as it comes across as very professional, as well as being very time efficient for them.

Dealing with Being Down-Valued

The result you dread could come through after the valuation, this is that the Valuer assigns a lower valuation to the property than you were requesting on the remortgage application. This is known as being *down-valued*.

For a remortgage, the Valuer will be looking for evidence that it is worth what you say you think it is worth. This needs to be supported with recent sales values of similar properties in the same area, or the value of improvement works you have had done to it since you bought it.

If the property is quite unique and hard to find other properties in the locality that directly compare with it, the Valuer may simply disagree with the price you are paying or the value you are asking it to be remortgaged against. This can be purely based on the Valuer's opinion concerning comparable prices and hence market value. This will be more of an opinion simply because there are no very close comparable property selling prices to work from.

One of the benefits of using a specific property type and particular location when investing using is that the more standard a property is in size and construction, the easier it will be to accurately predict the outcome of a valuation. This makes it harder for a Valuer to use any discretion, and they will have to follow the evidence of similar recent property sales values in the area.

With the more unique properties, it can feel like a real gamble getting it valued because you are really at the mercy of this opinion of the Valuer. You can challenge their opinion later, although in practice I have found it extremely hard to get a Valuer's professional opinion overturned.

With a remortgage, the main issue is that we are estimating a value for the property that we would like it to value up at. This differs from a property purchase where there is an agreed purchase price. The Valuer is likely to accept any reasonable offer price that has been agreed on as its true open market valuation, unless there are some good reasons found to dispute this. Although, as we should be serious investors buying at good prices compared to normal market values, this should not become an issue on purchase, or we are doing something wrong in the first place.

Generally, with a remortgage, you are at more risk that they may disagree with your estimated property valuation figure than if you were purchasing the property. For the rental valuation, this should not be such an issue, especially if you have rented it out and you can supply a copy of the rental agreement. This rental agreement is evidence of its rental value and you can also supply a rental comparable check for similar properties on the property rental portals.

The Valuer should also do their own work on rental price comparisons for similar properties. This may result in their opinion being that the market won't generally pay what you are claiming its rental value is worth, which may lead to a down-valuing situation based on rental value alone. This is because rental assessment can lower the overall loan value offered. It is not only the sale value of the property that is being assessed but also the rental value.

The rental income stress tests mean the rental income must cover more than a nominal mortgage interest rate by a specified percentage. Therefore, lowering the rental value could bring the cover below the threshold and therefore the loan amount offered will have to be adjusted accordingly.

If you are unfortunate enough to be down-valued by the Valuer's report, try to understand why so you can learn from it. It is unlikely you will be able to change the valuation once it has been published. It is like these seem to be set in stone once they have been issued, I have found.

There is a slight chance the Valuer could have made a mistake, such as missed out on some aspect of the property that should have been taken into consideration. Examples would be getting the number of bedrooms wrong by, for example, missing an attic bedroom out, or missing some useful outbuildings such as a garage or garden outhouse. In this case, there is a chance to appeal against the valuation through the lender. I am not aware of any other circumstances in which a lender will challenge the professional opinion of their Valuer, including simply the value they assigned to the property.

If you are still convinced that it is a mistake by the Valuer and that the property is truly worth more than the valuation report suggests, yet there is no error in the detailed account of the property in the report, your most realistic option is to go to a different lender for a different mortgage deal. Of course, I would expect that you had chosen the best deal available at the time. This means you might have to accept a mortgage deal not quite as good as the deal that you went for originally.

The Valuer from the new lender does not need to know about the fact that it has been valued recently by another valuer. Only check first that the new lender will not be sending out the same surveying company to do the valuation. Check this before committing to the remortgage application.

You can find out who the valuation company will be by asking your mortgage broker or the lender themselves. As a final check on this, the surveyors will need to contact you directly anyway in the event of a remortgage.

If you still get a similar valuation from a second different Valuer, you should challenge your own understanding of why you thought it should value up higher. You could find there is a learning point in there for you that will be a valuable lesson. We all make mistakes and this won't be the end of the world. Just take it positively and address any lessons learned in implementing your investing strategy, so you don't make the same mistake again.

Remortgaging Whilst Empty or Let?

As we have already commented upon, if you have the property let out then you can use the existing tenancy agreement as proof of rental income. Although this is a distinct advantage over stating what you believe you will be able to achieve for rental income, a let property also comes with the disadvantage that you are no longer in control of the condition and presentation of the property.

You might also have some problems getting access to the property, if you ended up with an awkward tenant in the house. This could make all your hard work come crashing down suddenly. I would therefore advise that you try to get the valuations done while the property is still empty. You might find this difficult if you have a smaller amount of work and a very efficient power team at getting the work done. That is because the property will be ready to let before you can apply for a remortgage after six months of ownership.

All I can say in this situation is that you should choose your tenant extremely carefully and maybe even visit them at their own current home to check how tidy they are. You don't want all your attention to detail being a waste of time when the Valuer comes and finds the place an absolute mess and he can't see all of the improvement work you have been focussed on.

Choosing Your Conveyancer

In order to carry out the remortgage, you will need to appoint a conveyancing solicitor. I would advise that you use a local solicitor for this rather than use an online service. I have used both and the online service eventually turned out to cost very much the same amount as the local solicitor.

The added advantage of a local solicitor is that you can use them for the purchases as well and you will likely be able to get a discount from them for repeat business that you will be doing during the BRRRR process. A local solicitor will also know the area better than an online solicitor's service and might be able to offer you some value at some point regarding advice on buying particular properties in the locality they are familiar with.

In theory, however, there is nothing that should go wrong with a remortgage using a solicitor that is not local to you, it is just that you miss out on the advantages of the personal service. Just like an online solicitor, you don't have to personally see them face-to-face if you don't need to. Any documents that need wet signatures can be witnessed by other people and not necessarily witnessed in the solicitor's office.

Insurance Value Increase

One of the other important things to come out of the remortgage valuation report is the *property reinstatement figure*, this is required for setting up the *buildings insurance* on the property. This is the estimated cost of the works to put the property back to the present state but to current Building Regulations. Don't be tempted to not declare or understate this to the insurer just to get cheaper insurance cover, in case you need to claim on the insurance policy in the future.

If you do not update or deliberately understate the reinstatement amount, any claim made in future could be reduced by the same percentage you undervalued the reinstatement figure by. There are some fixed tables that Valuers use to get this valuation figure, which is based on the floor area and property description. It is therefore best to go with whatever figure they provide you with on the valuation report.

When you remortgage, you should always go with the latest assessment of the insurance valuation, which will be on the valuation report for the remortgage. The difference can be just tens of pounds per year to upgrade to the latest estimate, but the risk factor of not doing so could be multiple thousands of pounds. My last insurance claim was for £50,000, and claims can of course be higher than that.

Note that the insurance value is not tied to the market value of the property, it is tied to the building trade costs for rebuilding the property. As such, I have found that I insure my properties for more than they are actually worth on the open market.

Drawing Down the Funds

The actual money provided to you by the lender, termed the *mortgage advance*, is the total money loaned to you. This includes any of the lender fees you agreed to be added to the loan and is therefore what makes up the opening mortgage balance. In contrast, the actual money sent to your conveyancing solicitor, termed the *drawdown*, is the money, less any added fees, that is available to contribute towards the purchase. This should be equivalent to the LTV percentage of the formal property valuation.

Before you can draw down the money however, you will need to sign the *mortgage deed* in the presence of a witness. They need to sign the document as witness and give their residential or business address. This cannot be a family member, so use a friend or business colleague, or even the conveyancing solicitor will do this for you if you prefer to keep your property matters more private. This mortgage deed is required to be signed for the solicitor to send on to the lender as proof of your acceptance of the contract you are entering into with them.

After this, your solicitor can agree on a date with the lender for the release of the money into their client account for you; this is in readiness to add to your deposit money and pay for the property. If it is a remortgage, the drawdown is used to pay off the original mortgage; any balance of funds left is then paid into your bank account. The money that is to be released to you will be shown on your solicitor's completion statement as funds owing to you.

With BRRRR, this transfer of funds from your remortgage conveyancing solicitor to your bank account is a key milestone. It should seal the process of the purchase using this approach because it should return to you the amount of money you have already invested into the project. That lines up for the next step in the process which is Repeat!

Be aware however that when your solicitor receives your mortgage drawdown money you will immediately start accruing additional interest. This will be payable either at the day of the month specified in the contract or one month from the date of the drawdown, as specified in the small print.

Banking the Money

This is a simple matter of requesting that the solicitor transfers the balance owing to you to an account of your choosing. The bank account you give to them will ideally be one that you have dedicated to the business of BRRRR and not mixed in with your daily living accounts. You don't want to be tempted into spending what is your seed capital on anything other than what you are focussed on achieving by building up your property portfolio using the BRRRR approach.

Congratulations on your investment property refinance!

Step Three of BRRRR(R!) completed.

If done correctly, you not only refinanced an investment property, you got all your invested money back out that covers all you have put into the property project, including your deposit money.

Rent

Loss of Full Control

Until the step of renting out the property, we have had full control over what we do with it. However, the moment you hand out the key to a tenant on an Assured Shorthold Tenancy Agreement, you have lost a lot of control over the asset and you are in the hands of the tenant until the tenancy is surrendered. In some unfortunate cases this might be a forced surrender by way of eviction proceedings, as is required for when the rent is no longer being paid by the tenant.

This step of renting is therefore very crucial to the overall success of your BRRRR model. Neither is it going to be a one-off item in the process as you are likely to have to rent your property out many times during your period of ownership. This of course means multiple risk-taking with the renting. But you have to rent the property out to generate the rental income to at least pay the mortgage interest payments.

Tenant vetting procedures are very important. This is especially so as you go down to the lower-income levels in my experience. As an example, I have many units that are rented to low income or benefit tenants, and for those I have had repeated issues over time with non-rent payment. However, I also have some professional let properties that I have never had a single rent default on. Where there has been a stoppage in rent payment it has always been caught up on later.

There is a logic behind this which I think is to do with the credit rating of the tenant. Professional tenants are more likely to guard their credit rating and need to deliver on their rent obligation to do that, for fear of county court judgement action. Whereas the lower-income tenants have more to gain by not paying their rent than they have with a good credit rating. I might be wrong but that is the only logic I have been able to put to it so far to justify my experience.

Not only have you lost control over whether you get any rent paid or not to a certain degree, but you have lost control over the condition of the property. All tenancies are supposed to allow for a reasonable amount of wear and tear which is for the landlord to put right in the end, usually at the end of the tenancy. However, there are often cases of accelerated degradation of a property which means you need to give it attention much earlier than you might have expected. It depends on the tenant.

In this respect, I have seen slower degradation in professional type lets, although don't expect them to keep the property up to the pre-let standard in the same way they keep their rent payments on track. At least that is my general experience overall.

Tenant Types

We have already discussed a full breakdown of the main tenancy types back in Chapter One, as we need to consider this in the first step when we buy. It could also be a factor in how we refurbish the property so it is more attractive to that particular tenant type we are aiming for. Or in another sense let's say it is not overdone to an amount that won't make any difference to the tenant type we are looking to attract. That is as long as we also get the best possible capital valuation for the property.

You might find different classifications of tenant types but the one I use is the one we have already discussed in Chapter One. You could get regional variations if there are particular niche letting requirements in your area. You should revisit the relevant section in Chapter One if you need a reminder of the tenant classifications I gave.

One of the key lessons I have learned is that it is hard to mix the different tenant types. This applies to single let housing where neighbours are concerned, should they be of a different tenant type. And more strikingly if you have a house in multiple occupation with different tenant types. Try to stick to what is the prevailing type that are occupying the neighbouring properties or rooms and that will make for a more peaceful life for you.

Matching tenant types will also give the benefit of longer tenancies which affects your profitability, as when a property is empty that is when it is damaging your profits most severely. There are therefore these two main benefits in matching up your tenant types. Hopefully, it will be to a level that will only take a day or so in the case of a professional let to put right again, but in the case of lower-income lets it can be weeks or even months of work. You might well feel you were back at square one again.

The above are however generalised statements, but ones that are grounded by experience. Other landlords will very likely tell you the same. Of course, the tenant type may also have a specific rent affordability level and you need to take that into account in setting your rent levels. You will have needed to have done that already back at the buying stage however, when planning ahead for the BRRRR process. It is too late and very reactionary if you are considering your tenant type and rental market at the stage of being ready to rent. That would not be a good approach to conducting your BRRRR business.

Property Management

Property Management can be taken care of by yourself or you can farm that out straight away to a rental agency. If you do it yourself, you will build up experience in dealing with tenants. You might find this experience useful for when you may later establish a rental agency to look after your properties and your employees might come to you for some guidance on certain matters. It does however take your focus away from the main business of building the portfolio, so it is an important decision to make.

I managed all my own properties in the first stages of setting up my property portfolio using BRRRR, however, it became quite demanding when I was also managing the refurbishment work and getting tenant matters to deal with at the same time. During that time, I learnt a lot about managing tenants and dealing with maintenance issues effectively. Personally speaking, I would not go back in time and change anything there. But you might be different; if that is the case then you will need to find a rental agency to look after your property for you.

If this is something you intend to do from the outset then you need to include the additional amount of money you will be spending on this service in your profitability calculations. This will more noticeably affect your net yield figure that we discussed in Chapter One.

However, there are hidden costs in using a management service that is hard to quantify and put into any calculation if you go this route. Nonetheless, you should be aware of what these are. Such hidden costs arise from the likely situation that letting agents will not manage your property as well as you would. At least not with the same interest at heart is what I mean, and not in the administration sense which is what they should be good enough to justify their fees. I have had a variety of agents manage my properties over the years but in the end, I have taken the properties back because I was not happy with their service in one way or another.

Therefore, don't just take it as read that the agent will manage your properties in the same manner as you would. Do you think they will feel as much pain as you when the rental income stops? Do you think they will be as keen to get you the best price for the maintenance work as you would? Do you think they will check on the quality of the maintenance work like you would, before paying for it? The answers to all these questions will materialise in either additional and unnecessary costs or a reduction in rental income.

By way of illustration, let me give you a short story about an agent that is nationwide in operation and growing in size. They acquired a small agency that was renting out a property that is located remotely from me. At the time of the takeover, I recognised the respected lettings agency name and was very comfortable it would be well managed. I was wrong.

One day I got a phone call from the agent telling me that the extraction system was not working and the new tenant wanted it fixed as soon as possible. They had therefore called out an electrician to look at it and told me it needed the main fan unit replacing with a price of around £350 fitted. You can add VAT to that as well, like the companies they work with normally have to charge on top of their actual charge of the work.

I was a little shocked as this was a job and cost I was not expecting. As it happened, I was to be passing by the apartment on the way to Manchester Airport the following day. I therefore called in and checked it myself to see what the problem was. I had a quick look and soon found that the isolator was not switched on because maybe the previous tenant did not like the sound of the extraction fan whirring, and had turned it off.

Maybe that is enough said about how using letting agents can be an issue, and that it is not just a matter of handing them the keys and taking passive income, like we would all like to believe it is.

Managing your tenants is of course a drain on your time and you could put a cost to that as well. That would be a notional cost as it would not come from your pocket but from your personal time. You could argue that it will still be more cost-effective to work with an agent as it stops you from working on the details inside your business and releases you to focus on the larger issues that could affect you in bigger ways regarding faster business development and more and better property deals being done.

I see both sides of the argument. For my journey, I took the self-manage approach until it was too large for me to manage alone. What is right for you might be a different thing, but I need to make the points for and against here so you can decide which way you will go in your BRRRR portfolio building strategy.

Advertising for Tenants

If you take the route of using a property management or rental agency to rent out your property then you won't need to worry about advertising as they will do this for you. All you need to keep an eye on is how long it is taking them to fill your property with a suitable tenant. If it is taking too long then you will need to look for another agent as it might be that the agent you are using is not good at attracting tenants for your type of property in the area you have invested.

When you manage yourself then you will be responsible for the advertising and taking the enquiry calls, as well as doing the viewings. Of course, you may have a partner helping you with this, or you may be doing it all yourself as I did, but the fact is you need to action it and reach out to potential tenants.

There are quite a few ways to advertise for tenants and you should not just rely on one approach. In the past, it was a matter of advertising in a local paper with a description of the property type and a rental price then just wait for the calls to come in. More recently the internet has taken over and the adverts need to be placed on internet locations like Gumtree as well as Facebook Marketplace and local Facebook groups by posting your advert on there, where that is allowed of course.

There are also specialist sites where you can pay to post your advert and it can also be posted out to the major internet rental portals for an additional fee. One such service is OpenRent that is currently used quite regularly by private landlords and that is a service we have been using recently to good effect for single lets. When it comes to advertising rooms then there are specialist websites such as Spare Room. You will need to test out what works best in your local area to generate a steady stream of enquiries for your vacant rooms or properties.

Setting the Rental Price
The rental price is determined by the market for the kind of property in the specific location it is situated in. Rental agents will have a good feel for this and it will help you if you look to see what they are advertising their rental properties at in the areas you have invested in, where the properties are similar.

As well as the condition of the property, the other factors that affect the rental price the most are the number and size of the bedrooms and any outside space available. Parking can help get a premium price if you have that in areas where it is not normal to have parking. Ideally, that would be garaged parking, but a private parking area will help you get more money simply because of the rarity of it. People who need or prefer this will be willing to pay for it.

Take account of the above factors when comparing local rental market prices in order to set your rental prices accordingly. If you happen to be using an agent then they will be advising you of the price to advertise at. It would be wise of you, in this case, to also do a check on what you think your property should command. Agents are more likely to advertise it at the lower end to get it through their books quickly, which you want also of course to get rental income coming in again. However, if you believe it is too low then you should ask them to raise it for you, which they will do on your instruction.

Where you have had a notice given by a tenant considerably well before their leaving, you can use that time to advertise at maybe a slightly ambitious rent and test the appetite of the market for the new value. You can then always lower it if there has been no interest shown before the time it gets critical to get a new tenant lined up.

For most rental markets outside of the more expensive area of London and the South East, it is quite normal to try rental changes in multiples of £25. You can always increase a monthly rent by say £75 for an ambitious increase, and then drop it by £25 each time you reduce to see at what level interest is shown. It seems that £25 can make a significant difference. In London and the South East, you might be looking at similar changes, but instead of monthly prices, you are looking at weekly rates with the same step changes!

If you are targeting a particular rental market you may well know what rent levels apply however. That would be typical of say the benefits claimants that are given a specific allowance for their rent payment and won't be able to go much above it no matter how good your property is. Given what we have already said about mixing tenant types, it would also not be an option to vary the tenant type too much to command a higher rent, even if the property would otherwise achieve it in a different location for example.

The most important thing in renting the property, with a good tenant assumed, is the rental occupancy level, the second most important thing is the rental price. One can affect the other, so make sure you are not hurting yourself by being too demanding on the rental value that you want to achieve. For example, if an extra £25 meant it took another month to rent the property, how many months will it take to get the money back for the income you lost with the missed one month's rent?

Tenancy Agreements

Tenancy agreements are necessary to formalise your contract with your tenant. However, you will only need to call on it if things go wrong. In theory, it should set out the terms of behaviour for your tenant, as well as outlining your obligations as their landlord. In practice, it is very much ignored by most tenants who might instead ask you about things that are already covered under the tenancy agreement.

You should however treat the tenancy agreement as seriously as possible at the outset to get the maximum benefit from having one. This will include sending them a draft copy to read well in advance of them coming to sign one. You can then reinforce that by asking them if they have any questions concerning the tenancy agreement or even clarifying some of the key points of the agreement in summary. This will be effective in pointing out exactly what you do and don't expect from your relationship with them as landlord and tenant.

This approach might have the effect of putting some tenants off, but it is more likely that those will be the kinds of tenants that you would prefer not to have. In that sense, the approach taken has already given benefits by screening the poor tenants out for you and keeping the opportunity open for attracting better tenants.

These are the kinds of details that will make BRRRR work, or cause it to fail if you don't have these or similar measures in place. If you use an agency to manage your property then you would do well to ask them how they ensure the tenants are taking the tenancy agreement seriously. If you are not happy with their answer, you can start to look elsewhere for a more suitable agent to switch to.

Rental Income Management

When you look at the theory of income generated for the BRRRR approach, it is assumed that the rental income magically appears in your bank account each and every month. The reality is that when you have a decent-sized portfolio then you have to be careful to monitor all rent payments as it is otherwise easy to miss a non-payer for a while.

It will be a matter of at least weekly focus on income profiles to be on top of matters. I have found that if they get away with you not contacting them straight away, it is more likely to end in tears for you and money in the pocket for them. Make sure you have an effective rental income management strategy as part of your BRRRR strategy focus.

I know some who go as far as making all the rent come in one specific day of the month so that they can have a major focus on who has not paid. Normally this will be the beginning of every month. New tenancies are taken on with the basis of paying the rent advance to also cover up to then next month's rent payment on a specific day.

Why do you think that some agencies managing their own properties would go to this extent if managing rent income is not otherwise a problem and a threat to their BRRRR strategy?

This is not to scare you but to point out the seriousness of managing rental income, which if not done will be the undoing and Achilles' Heel of the BRRRR system, even when all other things are done well.

Rent Payment Guarantees
You might already be aware that there are insurance services that offer rent guarantees. This is in exchange for a monthly insurance premium at a fraction of the rental income price. On the face of it these seem to be attractive for the BRRRR investor as the guarantee of income would give surety about covering the mortgage interest payments. Because of this, I have seriously looked at these but they seem to be only suitable for the professional type tenants where they have very good credit ratings.

In other words, they are only insuring the low-risk tenants in the first place. If I had a professional tenant not paying rent then I think the threat of county court action would be enough to force them to find the money from somewhere. I am therefore not using such rent guarantee schemes. I would be very interested in them if they were to cover the lower-income profile of tenant types, but unfortunately, that is not the case.

If you were thinking of using this to ensure your rental income for BRRRR, then you need to think again. Instead of having insurance policies, you will need to take action to guarantee your own income and that will come by taking prompt action when there is a late payment by contacting the tenant to inform them of the payment problem. It then needs to be escalated from there and going all the way to court for eviction proceedings if payment is not made in full.

As discussed before, the way you manage your tenant's rental payments will therefore be your best guarantee for typical BRRRR property and tenant types.

Tenancy Deposits

Tenancy deposits are the last bastion of keeping goodwill between a tenant and a landlord. Although the Government has made taking deposits about as hard as they possibly could, leading many landlords to wonder if it is worth the trouble of doing so.

The time and resources taken to register and manage the deposit is quite considerable and, because of this, there has been a reduction in the number of landlords taking deposits. This, in general, is a bad thing for the landlord as it means the tenant does not stand to lose anything should they damage something. It also means they are not bothered about the condition in which they leave the property. The only thing that could correct this behaviour without a deposit is if they think they will need some good landlord references in future.

If you do take a deposit from a tenant you need to do it in a correct way or risk being fined 3.5 times the amount of the deposit. This is on top of having problems getting your property back should you wish to take possession again. The correct way to do it can be quite time-consuming and heavy on administration. Some of the online rental agents have made this easier by automating some of these tasks. It is therefore advisable to use their services when taking deposits in my opinion.

In order to prove tenant damage and claim for it against a deposit payment, you will need to have very well documented evidence of the condition of the property at the point of letting. This should come in the form of a photo or video inventory and a written schedule of condition. Having these inventory reports done professionally and independently will be a good thing to do if you have a lot at risk with an expensive property or one that is furnished very extensively with high-value items.

When you come to the end of a tenancy, you can survey the condition of the property and put any costs forward to the tenant for a reasonable deduction to be made from the deposit paid. If they agree with you, all is well and good as they just electronically sign off on what you have agreed. They will then get their residual amount and you as landlord get the amount to cover the damages.

In claiming damages, however, you need to take into account the wear and tear of the goods, so you should claim a lesser amount than the cost of a replacement with a new item. This will not be considered however if the tenant agrees with what you are saying, it only becomes an issue if there is a disagreement and the matter has to go to independent arbitration. In this case, the points of view and evidence by both parties are submitted for consideration and the decision is made independently against which you cannot appeal.

In the more extreme cases of damage, I would even call it criminal damage. This is where the damage appears to be deliberate and extreme. There would be no way a deposit can cover this extent of the damage. You might have some cover by insurance in this case, if you have a policy that includes such matters.

There are even some buildings insurance policies that take this on and give you around £5,000 worth of cover for contents as well as the buildings cover. This would be for the fixed items at the property like the kitchen units and other fixtures and fittings.

In the case of such criminal damage happening, I have on some occasions contacted the police. I have done this in particular when this has been combined with the theft of items. If there is theft, it helps to have the serial number or other distinguishing markings recorded so that the police can go and retrieve the item from the tenant after leaving.

However, this can be quite an onerous thing to do, to have to keep a record of the serial numbers, therefore theft is often difficult to prove if you don't have this information available. Damage is easier to prove, but still a challenge and little hope of a successful deposit claim challenge if you don't have an inventory signed off by the tenant.

Property Condition Checks

Periodic property checks should be made and it is important to highlight this to the tenants at the start of the tenancy, in fact even when they are just considering the tenancy. If you manage to put them off by saying there will be some periodic property condition reporting then that will be all well and good as you might have deterred a poor tenant.

If you don't do any checks then you might not be aware of the rapid decline in the condition of your properties. When properties are not checked regularly then this is a possibility. When I say regularly, I mean about once every three months, so four times a year at a maximum. That should be sufficient to keep on top of things. It also gives chance to highlight any damage and have it repaired by the tenant, or at least at their cost.

In addition, you can spot any developing property problems that might have otherwise gone unreported by the tenant until it is a major problem. When a problem gets to this stage, it will be more difficult and more expensive to rectify. It will probably have caused other damage as well.

One case in point would be high-level water ingress, maybe simply from a blocked drain that needed clearing. In the end, there is plaster that needs replacing and a wall or two that needs redecoration, simply because it was not picked up early enough.

One of the downsides of doing these inspections is that it gives a tenant time to think of some small jobs that they would like doing. In your opinion, these might not be jobs that you should do but you might then feel obligated to do them as their landlord wanting to keep good relations with them.

Property inspections are definitely something that is going to be less problematic if you can get someone else to do these for you. That means if there is a request for some additional work then you are not put on the spot and having to answer to the tenant straight away. Instead, the problem report can be brought back to you and a very considered reply can then be given a little later on.

If you do send someone around to do the inspection, it might well be best to have someone who can fix small problems, like leaking taps for example. A handyman that can also carry out an inspection and document their findings would be ideal for this purpose.

If you have a rental agent managing your properties for you, then you simply need to get copies of the reports on a regular basis. The report should compare the property to the inventory and condition report which the tenant should have signed on taking up the tenancy. It will therefore highlight any degrading of the property as well as any problems arising. If there is evidence of excessive wear and tear or damage to the property then you can make plans to have this put right at the tenant's expense. The onus of proof will be on you of course, if the tenant contests it in any way.

Rent Arrears and Evictions

No matter how hard you try to manage your properties well, when you get to a reasonable portfolio size you are likely to have to take some serious action to protect the income that feeds your BRRRR investment model.

Rent being owed by tenants is likely to be an issue to you, unless you are renting solely to professional type tenants as we have discussed before. I explained how professional working tenants are very protective of their credit rating and are likely to ensure you are paid on time for your rent.

If you can manage to provide higher-end housing that gives a good yield with a professional worker as a tenant, you are generally in a good position as regards being paid your rent reliably. Unfortunately, the typical properties suitable for BRRRR are normally not attractive to the higher paid workers, and are more suited to the lower-income families and individuals.

If you are renting to social security claimants or sometimes working people who are in and out of work as a lifestyle, you are very likely to have serious rent arrears at some point. The level of arrears will depend a lot on how you manage it, but the fact is you will be owed money. This is a fact of renting and a battle you will have to face at some point, even if you are lucky enough for it not to be a regular occurrence.

In dealing with getting the rent money owed to you, you will of course have to try to deal with it by direct communication with the tenant to remind them to pay. You can then escalate this with a demand for payment by a certain date. You can next threaten eviction if no payment is made leading to the issuing of a Notice to Quit. If still no payment is made, it can take on a life of its own that may lead to court action being taken and finally a bailiff to enforce the eviction.

Outside of this, you have other options to get your money, albeit these options are not as effective as these should be to protect landlords. However, as we discuss elsewhere, protection of landlords' income is not something that is on the agenda of those who make and pass the housing laws we have to deal with.

One option you will have is to call in a private debt collector who can then take on the case. You can also submit the case to a solicitor who can write them letters and threaten the action of eviction at a further cost. In my experience, the private debt-collectors action is largely ineffective and I would be very careful who you set on to do this for you.

Solicitors serving notices is not something I can comment on as I have not done this due to costs for sending letters out and the likelihood of response from the tenant types I have. However, if you can find a solicitor who will do this for you at a reasonable cost, this could be an option. Even if it is an empty threat in that you would not go ahead with the action through the solicitor, it might still have the desired effect.

There are also private organisations focussed on debt recovery from tenants and who will also take it all the way through to eviction. In these cases, you should expect to pay handsomely for their services, which will add to your out-of-pocket situation. But you may get lucky and get some money from the tenant if they use their powers of persuasion carefully enough. This is a rare event, but it can happen.

There is another option that used to be very effective and I have used it many times in the past. This is 'money claim online', and if you Google that phrase, you can get all of the details. I have used it to good effect in the past after discussions to obtain the rent money failed. I have also had county court judgements awarded solely by using this approach.

However, in recent years I have found out that it is more difficult to implement in that you have to provide a very good record of all the attempts to claim the money before you make the claim. You will need to show detailed records of what you have done and the judge will have to be happy that nothing else could be done. This was not so onerous in the past, and it is a shame that it has now got to this difficult-to-enforce level.

When you go to court with a Section 8 Notice to Quit, you will get an award of the rent arrears on the judgement if you are successful with your case. This is a County Court Judgement (CCJ) that will be recorded against the tenant. You won't be able to claim all the costs involved in taking the matter to court, but some costs will be awarded on top of the rent owing.

Whichever claim route you go down, once you have the court order, you need to implement it and that is an entirely different story and not an easy matter to force payment. It might be that the tenant or ex-tenant will pay you to remove the CCJ from their credit file, although in my experience this is often not the case. It will expire after six years anyway, but in the meantime, they will have to deal with any credit searches that show this debt on public record.

Having a good system for protecting your rental income and one that goes all the way to eviction proceedings in court is a necessary part of your tools to keep your BRRRR system alive and well.

Rental Risks

As stated in the opening passages of this chapter, once you start to rent out your property you lose direct control over your property. This opens you up to significant risks that you need to manage. We have already discussed some of what these are concerning the degrading condition of the property and the risk of not getting the rental money you are owed each month. These two factors are the most common in my experience and you will do well to focus on reducing the possible adverse impact of these in your BRRRR management system.

I have covered all the other main negative factors associated with renting out property in my second book *UK Property Investment: The Toxic Truth!* This was a book meant to highlight many of the negative aspects of property investment that never seem to be openly spoken about, at least not by those promoting property investment of course. However, I felt the truth had to be told so I wrote that book as a warning for anyone considering entering property investment.

Some of the feedback that I got on releasing that book was to do with it being focussed on Buy to Let and not property investment in general. That is true, but most investment that is done in property in the UK is for buying to let. The other areas of property investment, such as property developing and trading by flipping properties, is very small in relation to buying to let.

In respect of BRRRR, the risks highlighted in that book provide an extremely good fit, as this is a system that focusses on buying to let. You might therefore be interested to read the risks highlighted in that book if you want a thorough grasp of this area. I am not trying to scare you away from using BRRRR, but I think you should have the benefit of my experience offered up in a very honest and open way.

I will however highlight here some of the additional risks below which are also presented in that book. This will at least give you a flavour of what may lie ahead. To be forewarned is to be forearmed as they say.

It might seem hard to imagine, for many people, that interest rates could rise sharply. This would in fact destroy the investing model of most people in the modern property investment world. Of course, for those with fixed rate mortgage deals, there would be protection from this during their fixed-interest period. For those with variable-rate mortgages, the hit would be sudden and quite drastic. In a sense, we are gambling on interest rates staying low when we are on a variable-rate interest mortgage. I have many of these mortgages, but also some fixed-rate mortgages as a hedge.

In 2007 the base rate was at 5.5% and this made most standard variable rate mortgages around 7.5%. This fell drastically in 2008 when the financial crisis struck and since then it has never returned to such higher rates. However, the long-term average of the Bank of England base rate is about 5%. We are now in an unprecedented low interest-rate environment and it is probably something that many investors have never known to be any different.

Shocks to the world and its economy however are clearly something we might now come to anticipate. Fortunately for investors, when the economy is not doing very well, there is a tendency for the interest rates to be set low. However, the main tool that is used to help control inflation is the Bank of England base-rate of interest. This means if something initiated a sudden increase in inflation, interest rates would very likely have to be increased to control it.

I remember when I first started investing, I was meeting people who were reminding me that interest rates only a few decades earlier or so had been at 15%, in an effort to control rising inflation. This led to a lot of property repossessions at that time and people struggling to keep hold of their homes.

There were many people buying properties for investment even back then, and those I knew had to exit the market as they had taken out finance in some way to help make their purchases. This was at a time just before buy-to-let mortgages were available and so commercial finance had to be used. This would include the additional pressure of paying back the capital and doing so over a shorter period than is often associated with a typical mortgage term.

A sudden increase in interest rates is therefore something that could happen again, even though I can't imagine the circumstances upon which a sudden increase in rates would be triggered. However, we have had events recently that have put the world into lockdown that we also could not have imagined just six months prior. Things can change quickly and uncontrollably.

Borrowing money to buy investment properties therefore carries the risk of an increase in cost that you cannot be fully in control of, and BRRRR very heavily relies on this. It could therefore be a major threat to your investment empire you may have built up over the years. This might be very unlikely, but at the same time, entirely possible. The way to mitigate this risk is to pay down the capital on the mortgages to reduce your gearing. This will have to come from business profits or income from outside of the BRRRR activity.

In the time I have been investing in property now, I have also seen a vast increase in the amount of legislation introduced to make owning and letting out property much more onerous. And this is just in a space of less than two decades, with more legislation reported to be on the horizon. It seems relentless.

When I first started, at the turn of the new century, buy-to-let was the talk of the town. All we had to do from a contractual point of view was get a tenancy agreement signed. You then had the right to claim your property back if there were any issues with the tenant behaviour, or simply because you want it back. Nowadays we have to make sure there are many boxes ticked before doing that (even though you own the property), including demanding routes to registering and protecting any tenant deposit paid.

We could also charge for the administration involved in registering the new tenant to cover the costs of our time or the time or services of others (including taking references and credit checks). Recently, even this changed and despite the increase in the documentation required, the costs for covering such extensive tenancy set-up activity cannot be charged to the prospective tenant anymore.

You will need to absorb this increased administration and any future demands as part of daily business. Increasing your rental prices will be the best way to mitigate this, that way you can afford to pay for the extra work and other associated costs. The flip side of increasing your rents is that you don't want to increase your void periods, this relationship of the rental price to void period has already been discussed.

One of the next items on the Government's agenda is further increasing the demands for thermal efficiency of a home. The housing stock typical for purchase by BRRRR strategies will be hardest hit as most of these houses were built around 1900 and significant upgrades will be required to achieve the espoused EPC grade C. If there is no significant financial support from the Government to achieve this, that will be a huge capital cost for the BRRRR landlord.

As already mentioned, when George Osborne was Chancellor, he brought in his "anti-landlord tax" (often more formally referred to as the Section 24 landlord tax), this was done at the same time as the 3% surcharge on stamp duty for second homeowners. The only difference was that the anti-landlord tax was phased in over 4 years; this seems to have been an attempt to slow cook you so you don't notice it until it is too late. In many cases that has worked and has caught some landlords out with a big tax problem.

This gradual introduction tactic shows the Government knew it would have a significantly adverse effect on landlord financials. In Northern Ireland, this same punitive tax was brought into full effect overnight in times past but then was repealed as the effect was so devastating on landlords who were exiting the market. The UK Government, therefore, learned from that and craftily brought it into the rest of the UK over four annual stages.

This introduced a massive change to the tax allowance on finance expenses used to purchase properties. It effectively disallows interest on landlord finance costs (mostly mortgage interest for landlords) and simply replaces it with a 20% tax credit. This step therefore specifically targets the higher and additional rate taxpayers.

This tax is solely targeted at landlords owning properties in their personal name and using mortgages, as well as other sources of finance to acquire their properties. The other thing to be aware of with this tax is that you have your fictitious 'profits' not only taxed, but also added to your other sources of income. That means even if you are a basic rate taxpayer, the interest you pay on the mortgages could put you in the higher rate tax bracket for no increase in actual disposable income.

In answer to this tax, most landlords are now looking to form limited companies, amongst other business structures, with which to purchase and/or hold their portfolio of properties. This however can cost a lot of money for existing landlords as in some cases they have to effectively 'sell' their properties into a company and pay the associated taxes. Other ways around this are being sold by tax advice businesses, although there are risks there about possibly falling foul of the General Anti Abuse Regulations (GAAR); meaning if this is done solely to save tax, it can be disallowed.

Therefore, new landlords are often advised to simply form a limited company in which to hold the properties to avoid this additional taxation. However, who is to say the Government won't soon bring in the same regulations for property investment businesses. This tax was applied retrospectively to landlords owning in their own name, so the Government could later do the same to property companies.

Even after operating your property business inside a limited company, you will face double taxation in terms of paying corporation tax before taking money out of the business as profits in dividends. Let alone forgetting the fact there is no personal capital gains tax allowance available upon disposal of any property when owning property inside a limited company.

You should therefore take tax advice on your investment plans from a tax adviser that is well-versed in property taxes. Otherwise, this could be a threat to your BRRRR system, even if it only evidences itself some years down the line.

I hope that has given you food for thought on some of the main risks that could threaten your BRRRR investment model and some ideas on how to counteract those risks. If you want to learn more about other related risk factors, you have the name of my second property book to look up and read at your leisure.

Property Legal Obligations

If you researched the amount of legislation that applies to a landlord that is currently in force, you would be horrified. Nevertheless, ignorance is no excuse and you will have to educate yourself on this subject. Even if you give the task to an agent, the responsibility remains with you to ensure legal obligations are complied with.

I can only give you a very brief summary here as to what are the main topics, I think this would need a book in its own right to do the subject justice. However, a summary might be useful if you are new to property investing and starting out with the BRRRR approach.

It is also important to be aware that some of the duties carry the potential for a criminal prosecution, if not complied with. This is heightened if you go down the Houses of Multiple Occupation route, as I have done.

You will need to have smoke alarms installed and working on each level of the property. These need to be proven to be operational when the tenant takes up occupancy so you might want to get them to sign to say this is the case. These don't have to be interlinked and hard-wired smoke alarms but that would be the best practice to consider. The next requirement that is on the horizon at the time of writing is to have carbon monoxide alarms installed as well. This is something many landlords do in any case already, just for peace of mind.

The electrical system will need checking and certifying by a qualified electrician every five years. This has only recently been introduced although in the past there was a requirement to ensure that the electrical system was safe. How they expected most normal landlords to ensure this is beyond me, but that is the law. In fact, that is still in place in addition to the five-yearly checks so you need to at least do a visual check between each let to make sure there is nothing obviously wrong with the electrical system.

Portable appliance testing is required for any small electrical appliance that is left in a house as part of the letting inventory. If you do furnished-lets, this can be a significant amount of testing needing to be done annually. In some cases, landlords have educated themselves on how to use portable appliance testers and do this themselves. You can take courses on how to do this and how to register and record the findings to keep the required register of portable appliance testing.

The furniture used in the property needs to comply with fire regulations and therefore you need to be careful of any second-hand furniture you put in to furnish a property. As these regulations date back to 1988, it is now probable that most furniture that would be available second hand will comply. However, you need to confirm this and check for the label that states compliance.

Annual gas safety checks are required on any gas appliance in a rented home. This would include gas fires, gas hobs and ovens, as well as the gas boiler. This must be done by a registered Gas Safe engineer and a certificate issued and given to the tenant, or posted up in the house in the case of HMOs.

At the time of writing, to legally rent out a property, it must have an Energy Performance Certificate and the rating needs to be E or above. This requirement is however only on an upward trajectory and discussions are underway to increase it to a C. As I have already covered, this would be very demanding for rental stock typical of a BRRRR investor. Recently, the local councils have been using the EPC register to spot any properties that are not in compliance and then threatening landlords with fines for not renting out suitable homes fit for rental purposes.

In addition to the increasing legislation required for rental housing stock, there also seems to be an increase in tenants' rights. Shelter and the Citizens' Advice Bureau appear to be the main pressure groups pestering the Government for the changes that result in more tenants' rights and more legal matters for landlords to deal with.

In my experience, a tenant that pays well will also speak good about you as a landlord, but the many that don't pay well will call you all the names under the sun. The logic I put to this is that it makes them feel better for their tenant wrong-doings. Whereas, those not doing any wrong can only see good in you.

A poor-paying tenant is therefore likely to give a bad account of their landlord to the representatives of the pressure groups. The reality is that the landlord may have been nothing of the sort as described. The matter was an attack on the landlord without them being able to defend themselves. The root cause being that the tenant was behind on rent and maybe wanted to move from their present premises simply because of that and start again.

The people in the pressure group organisations believe the tenant's lies (or at the very least, their exaggerations). It gets formalised through written reports and stories and makes most landlords look bad. Landlords are then judged without a hearing. I don't claim that all landlords are good but the vast majority I know only want to do the best they can for their tenants.

There is only a small minority who want to exploit tenants. Some local landlord's names who I don't know personally, keep cropping up concerning this topic. However, you will get good and bad in all businesses, not just property; although it seems landlords all get tarred with the same brush as far as these pressure groups go. There is no end to this tenant-strengthening legislative onslaught in sight, be prepared for further tightening in the near future.

The main one that is already on the agenda is to abolish the Section 21 notice to quit. This is a notice that a landlord can serve to get possession back for a property they own and without giving a reason. The pressure groups have complained to the

Government and said that landlords use this notice to get revenge on tenants who complain to them. These are framed as so-called revenge evictions.

In my experience, I have only known these notices to quit be used because these notices are the most-sure way to get your property back, simply because you don't have to prove anything in court except that you own the property. For example, when you have problems with antisocial behaviour complaints or drug-related problems at the property. If you were to take a fault-based Section 8 notice to quit route you would have a considerable burden of proof to fulfil.

Landlords have also used Section 21 notices to remove non-paying tenants as it is a more-sure way to get your property back than using Section 8 eviction proceedings for rent arrears. I am not aware of any landlord who has used it simply because a tenant is complaining about a repair requirement that has not been attended to, as a revenge eviction. That seems to be an exaggerated claim, but you can see that it leads to legislation that can give landlords other problems now.

You therefore need to keep abreast of the changes in legislation that is not only affecting your property standards but also how they give rights to tenants. These can both result in additional costs to your property business that you will need to finance in one way or another.

Congratulations on the Rental of your investment property!

Step Four of BRRRR(R!) completed.

If done correctly, you not only rented your investment property, you get regular rental income that more than covers your mortgage interest payments and other expenses, then you take the money left over as profit.

Repeat

Repeat What?

The most obvious repeat of course is to go back to Step One and buy another property. That certainly is the primary repeat, and the only step you can repeat straight after the purchase of your first investment property. When you see the word Repeat in the BRRRR process this is effectively what it is referring to.

There are however other things you will need to regularly repeat. Even if you only stayed with the one investment property, the R for Repeat will still apply to you. This is not something that is mentioned very often but it is a fact that you need to repeat several of the steps of the BRRRR process going forward. From the discussion so far, you will probably have already picked up on these repeat requirements.

We will now go through those repeating steps here in this chapter for more clarity on the topic. This will help you to understand more fully what is required by Repeat in the BRRRR investment strategy. Although it might not be exactly what you think it meant. (I don't think the originators of the acronym BRRRR thought of it this way either! However, this is the reality of it.)

Repeat Property Purchasing

Repeating the property purchasing process is something that should have already started even before you were ready to purchase another property. By this, I mean before you had the cash back in the bank from the refinance to be able to purchase again. If you are lucky, you might even have enough money in the bank, or accessible by other means, to repeat another purchase even before you have completed the refinance on the first property.

This is the best situation to be in where you have two or more investment pots to work with, rather than just the one which is normally the topic and focus the straight forward BRRRR process. This means that you can be completing on the purchase of the next property before you have even completed the refurbishment work on the present property if you want to.

You need to get the timing right here though, because I have had situations where I have had two properties newly purchased and needing refurbishment, which then dilutes your focus on the job at hand. It is better to have a focus on one property refurbishment at a time, especially if you are doing this with just yourself at the helm, as will be the case for most investors.

Irrespective of whether you have two investment pots of money available or not, you will need to have your next property lined up for completion as close as you can to the refinancing and letting out of the present property you are working on. This will govern the speed at which you will grow your portfolio. In addition, because it is not a quick and simple matter to find a suitable property purchase at the right price that suits the BRRRR model, you will need to spend time looking for the next property during the work on the present property.

This is often referred to in property investing circles as having your deal pipeline. You should offer on properties even if you don't have the funds at the time. You will need to show evidence of funds to progress with the purchase but you could mention the refinance that is imminent if you need to do so. That would show that you have the funds available shortly.

For an estate agent that will not be acceptable however, unlike if you are dealing with a vendor direct who may well accept this and start the conveyancing based on the promise of the funds being available ready for completion. However, even with the estate agent you will have had your offer put forward to the buyer since they only ask for proof of funds when you have had the offer accepted by the vendor. This will give you a good feel for the present market, even if the outcome is that the offer is subsequently refused if you can't substantiate where the cash needed for the purchase will be coming from.

In some cases, you may have had an offer refused, but then later when the deal falls through with another investor, they might come back to you with your first offer to see if you are still interested to buy. That timing might just tie in well with the refinancing of the present project you are working on so you can offer to take the deal on. In this way, you feed your pipeline and you should get offers accepted coming out of the end.

The buying activity in terms of looking for suitable properties never ends. That is even though on the BRRRR sequence it seems you have to Repeat and go back to the beginning stage of Buying only after refinancing of the present property. We have already covered a summary of how to look for properties for sale right at the beginning of Chapter One, so I won't repeat those tips here again. It is however those things that need to be constantly running for as long as you are building your property portfolio.

Repeat Property Refurbishments

Having spent some time going through the requirements for renting out your property in the last chapter, you will probably have noticed my repeated reference to the downgrading of property condition over time. In particular that this can happen quickly or more slowly depending on the category of tenant and also the tenant themselves in particular.

When I look at the BRRRR model it comes across as a linear step-by-step approach. However, although it is not easy to show in a sentence containing letters, there should be loopback arrows from some R's back to another R. In particular there needs to be a large arrow looping back from Rent to Refurbish. I once omitted this arrow unknowingly and ended up in a terrible position of not being able to rent out my property to decent tenants. This initiated a downward spiral that you will do well to avoid.

In fact, this was also coupled with me venturing out on a step that I have already warned should be taken with care. That is to rent out using a rental agent. I will give you the story here so that you might be able to appreciate how this can occur and also appreciate the importance of keeping your properties in good condition, no matter what type of tenant you are renting to.

This is a very general statement, but one that is borne out in my experience. It is a fact that letting agents will not manage the property as well as you would. At least not with the same interest at heart is what I mean, and not in the administration sense which is what they should be good at to justify their fees. I have had a variety of agents manage my properties over the years but in the end I have taken the properties back, because I was not happy with their service in one way or another.

The longest relationship I had with an agent was, in fact, an agent that worked as part of the local council. I was sure that they must be able to look after my properties better than I could. During my time with this agent, I was working abroad and gave the management of my properties entirely over to them for a period of around four or five years. When I took the properties back, I was shocked at the condition of them and each one needed pretty much a full refurbishment.

During the time they were managing the properties for me I was also sent quite a lot of bills for maintenance work done at each of my houses. These were not insignificant bills either, to put it mildly. Based on the level of the bills, I was fairly sure that things were being kept up on the maintenance side. In addition, the properties were being filled quickly enough so there was no cause for concern.

However, after about three years, the time taken to fill the properties was getting longer and longer, whilst the tenant problems and issues were increasing with each subsequent let. I was getting concerned. Also, the rent payment record was getting worse and worse. It got to a point where I had to step in. When I did that, I was shocked at the condition of the properties and realised there was no way I could get a decent tenant until a refurbishment was done at each property.

I confronted the agent about why the properties were so run down and the answer floored me; he said they were trying to save me money! Really? Not according to my bank account on maintenance costs. Not according to the length of the void periods. Not according to the poor payment record of the poor tenants that they were only able to sign up on my behalf.

In the end, I had no other option but to take the properties back and bring them under my management again when I returned to work in the UK. Not that I wanted to do this, but I would otherwise be losing a lot of money month after month. If you are a landlord with a considerably sized portfolio, which is what we are aiming for in

BRRRR, you may find recovering from this situation very difficult as you have a lot of refurbishments required all at the same time.

I hope this story illustrates two points. Firstly, to keep on top of any agents you use that are renting your properties for you. You can do this by asking to view the condition before each new letting. (That was not so easy for me as I was working abroad at the time, but maybe I could have asked for photos or video tours). The second point is that no matter who manages your properties, you need to keep on top of the condition of the property.

After each rental you will be looking at a minor facelift of the property to at least the standard it was let out in. If you can claim some deductions from a bond to help then all the better, but in any case, you will need to do this to keep from losing rental income by increased voids and a reduced quality of tenant.

Repeat Property Rentals

In order to keep the income coming in it will be necessary to keep the property rented. Depending on the tenant type, property location, condition of the property, as well as the tenant themselves, this could be a regular repeating matter say between six months to two years typically. Now if you think about when you have umpteen number of properties that are all on such a frequency of changeover, I think you get the picture.

You will likely not just be advertising one property for rent but several properties at any one time. That comes with the associated work for refurbishment at least before allowing a viewing on one that needs some attention. You can keep photos of the time before it was last let out, to enable you to visually advertise it for rent before it is available again. That will build up a pipeline of tenants interested in the property, although you might well need to do at least a touch up of the property before letting it out again.

Upon a notice being received by a tenant that is leaving, you can arrange a visit either by you or someone you work with, to check on the condition. That will give you a good idea as to whether it is worth advertising it to rent before it is empty again or not. In some cases, you might even ask the present tenant if they will allow some viewings before they leave. This is of course only where the property has been well looked after and is being kept in a tidy condition that would appeal to prospective tenants.

Maybe you can see that as you build up your property portfolio, this will become more of a full-time job for you or someone else and you should plan towards making that so. In many cases with landlords who are growing in size, they will start their own rental agency. This will be mostly for their own properties, although it helps in several areas if you can also rent out some properties for others.

We have already discussed the process as well as many topics regarding effectively dealing with renting out properties in Chapter Four. You will need to apply those principles to your repeat rental activity and build up systems to implement these in a reliable and repeatable way.

Repeat Property Refinancing

Repeated refinancing brings on additional demands as you become what is known to lenders as a portfolio landlord. When you own a small portfolio of properties there may be some lenders that do not want to lend to you anymore and those that do will require more information on your present portfolio before they do. That will reduce the pool of lenders available which means you will have less scope for getting the best mortgage deals on offer.

It only takes ownership of four financed investment properties to be classed as a 'portfolio landlord'. In fact, when you apply for your fourth investment financing, that is when the additional requirements will hit you. In September 2017, the Prudential Regulation Authority (PRA), which is an arm of the Bank of England and regulates mortgage lenders, issued new guidance to lenders on how they should assess mortgage applications for portfolio landlords.

In general, from a PRA and most lenders' point of view, for an investment property to count towards this status, it needs to be mortgaged, or have some secured lending registered against it. This includes any homeowner residential mortgage with a 'consent to let' awarded against it and any 'holiday let' properties with secured borrowing.

Properties owned either in the applicant's personal name or via a company owned by them will be counted, as will any properties that are in joint ownership with someone else. However, any foreign property owned by the applicant will not be taken into account.

With the status of 'portfolio landlord', there are more stringent application requirements for obtaining any further mortgage borrowing, as recommended by the PRA. A portfolio landlord will, therefore, have to provide much more information about their investment and financial situation than someone new to property investment.

Each lender has its own particular requirements and format for information presentation. However, in general, the portfolio landlord will need to demonstrate at least two years' landlord experience, provide SA302 tax returns for the last full two years, provide three months account statements showing rental payments, and give a schedule of properties with associated borrowing details, and even provide a basic business plan to set the current investment decision in context. This is in addition to the usual information requested by lenders for all applicants.

Once this information has been prepared, it can easily be updated for future borrowing applications as a portfolio landlord, so the provision of this additional information does not become too onerous. However, as it needs to be up to date, make sure you have your SA302 tax return submitted and approved as soon as you can, at the end of each tax year. Typically, for any new application, a lender will need this completed and accepted by HMRC by the September following the close of the latest tax year. Therefore, any new borrowing requests from September onwards will likely need the latest SA302 to accompany the application.

When you have four investment properties, you are likely to face the first limitation on the number of lenders available to you. Some lenders will have a limit on lending to you for just four properties in total. It will not be so dramatic at this stage, but you should be aware that this is the case. It comes as a surprise to those who are not aware of this and think they can keep getting the same deal from one of the lenders who have this lending criterion in place.

The next level of portfolio lending restrictions I have noticed is when you get to ten properties. At this stage, the reduction in deals is more noticeable. You will likely not be able to get access to some of the very best interest rate deals available. The reason for this is that you are seen as a higher risk to the lenders on defaulting on your mortgage payments. The higher rates are therefore the only ones available to reflect this additional risk level.

I have seen some marked differences in what is available for landlords with fewer than ten properties to those with ten or more. The interest rates that I saw for those with fewer than ten were approximately half of the rate of those on offer for landlords with ten or more properties. This can have a huge effect on your operating costs and so you should consider this carefully when projecting the growth of your property business as regards the cost of finance going forwards

In the longer term of borrowing money, it is unlikely that you will stick with the same lender and the same mortgage product for the life of the loan. When you take out each mortgage it will normally be an agreement for 20 – 25 years, or maybe 30 years in some cases. However, it is unlikely you will stay with the lender on the same product for that period of time.

The reason for this is that more attractive mortgage loans will become available and it might well be too expensive to stick with the present mortgage deals. When you take out another mortgage you will restart the lending period again. That will be especially so if you are taking on interest-only mortgages, which are more typical of the type you will use as a BRRRR investor.

As you stay in the property game for a longer period, there should be a rise in property prices. The amount of time that this takes will depend on at what stage you invested in the property price cycle. For some, it will be a matter of just a few years to see significant growth, for others it may be over a decade. It also depends on the area you invest in. For example, the North has seen much slower house price growth over the last decade than the South has.

With the BRRRR approach, this will effectively lower your gearing levels without you having to pay off any of the mortgages. During this time the property rental prices should have increased as well which reflects the house price growth. You then have an opportunity for another Repeat to help you. It is still a repeat Refinance, but not one to help with releasing money anymore.

In the past when there was rapid house price growth, buy-to-let investors would happily release the capital in the properties through refinancing. However, that is taking a short-term view and although it puts money in your pocket now you have to pay the price of increased interest payments later. There is however a smarter thing to do that will make our BRRRR life much easier and more quickly lead you towards the final 'R' for retirement.

This refinance stage should therefore simply be to put you onto a lower rate of interest to reduce your outgoings and make the whole financing of your portfolio easier. This should result in releasing money you can live on for your retirement. At least that is the amount of money that you have planned to take from property income in retirement (you should have other forms of retirement income as well). This is a great opportunity because the mortgage payments are likely to be the highest single outgoing on your investment property so it can make a significant difference.

In fact, the difference between mortgage payments between one mortgage and another can make the difference between making money or not on a mortgaged investment property. This is because the range of payments between different mortgage deals can vary so significantly.

A lower Loan to Value (LTV) generally offers better interest rates due to the lower risk to the lender. Of course, if you do nothing then your present lender would continue to charge you at the rate agreed for the LTV you had when you first took out the mortgage with them. This is even though they will be offering lower interest rates for lower LTV ratios. These significantly lower rates start to really take effect at around 65% LTV. Since you may well have started at around 75% LTV, it won't take long before you will be eligible for a cheaper interest rate mortgage, and you should take that opportunity.

Of course, you have to take into account all the costs of remortgaging to make sure it saves you significant money overall. However, a review of your mortgage position when you have had a significant increase in the value of your investment property can very likely lead to saving significantly on monthly mortgage costs by remortgaging.

You can consider this also if you have some spare money that you are not requiring for your on-going property investment. It is probably going to give a better payback when used in this manner than it will in the bank, especially given the present savings interest rates.

You will do this by taking a lower loan amount and then making up the difference by putting money into the conveyancing process to pay off the balance owing on settling the loan amount currently outstanding with the present lender. BRRRR investors generating spare cash from maybe property teaching, mentoring or selling-on deals, will probably be doing this to increase the security and profitability of their BRRRR portfolio.

Of course, it is still in your interest to get the property valued up as high as possible to give you the highest loan at the lowest LTV, therefore it would make sense to do any cosmetic upgrades before the valuation. You can do this even with a tenant still in place; I am sure most tenants would have no objections to a property upgrade for free!

In fact, it would of course make sense to invest some of your available money into ensuring that you get the best chance of the highest possible valuation on remortgaging. The money you put into this will be classed as payment for repair work for tax purposes and therefore can be fully offset against income to reduce your tax liability.

In particular, you should upgrade your investment property if you have an opportunity of a period with no tenant coming up around a time where you could consider remortgaging. In this case, it is worth taking that opportunity to do more extensive cosmetic upgrade work than would be possible with the tenant in place. We are mostly talking about decorating here and of course any obvious visual repairs for damage to walls and surfaces for example. Maybe also doing some work to give a facelift to kitchens and bathrooms and replacement of any fixtures and fittings that are showing signs of wear.

With the best possible clean and fresh appearance, this is highly likely to influence the valuation in a positive direction. It is, however, still your duty on a remortgage to state your expected valuation figure. This refresh and upgrade work should give you the confidence to give a figure very much on the higher side of what would be considered reasonable.

Repeating Learning Cycles

Each of the repeating activities should also present a learning cycle where you are getting better at each one. When I say *better,* I am referring to anything that improves the bottom-line profitability. These can come from many varied sources that all add up and as you improve in each area of repetition it should feed down into your profitability.

If you are not open to learning and simply keep on doing things as you have always done them, you will be missing out on this additional profitability potential. Learning should also be interesting so it will add to the personal value of what you do in your BRRRR activities. Look for learning opportunities especially in things that don't go right, or lead to a lesser outcome than you had expected. If you can learn from any mistakes so you don't repeat them, that alone will bring you value going forwards.

Examples of learning from repetition would be buying properties with better potential for an uplift in value than the ones that you first bought. As you learn and view more properties and carry out more refurbishments, you will quickly learn where you can make step increases in the value of the property.

As one specific example, I soon learnt that a master bedroom in a terraced house that has an area which is located directly above the landing of the stairs leading up to the first floor included in its floor space, can soon be adopted as a small ensuite. Often these were being used as small storage spaces or acting as wardrobes. Depending on the size of the area, I might have to extend it slightly but even by doing so it would not take much of the overall bedroom area up. I then started to look out for this as an opportunity in the properties that I was viewing.

Another area of learning comes from repetition in refinancing where you should be finding the better deals that come along to get the best financing option. Your repetition of working with your mortgage broker will help you in this as they better understand what you are doing and offer to help you. Your repeat business will make you a higher priority customer and they will look to do as best they can to secure your repeat business for the foreseeable future.

Learning through repeat renting will be a long and continuous learning curve. You will probably also have to adapt to different markets as things change. Originally, I started out focussing on letting to benefit claimants, but that had to change when changes to how benefits were paid made that a much more challenging sector. Instead of paying landlords direct for benefit claimants then it went to the tenant first, which brought on additional challenges I was not equipped to face, nor wanted to deal with.

After that, I moved on to housing for migrant workers coming to the local area to work. As you can see, that is all change again now with Brexit taking place and so you have to learn a different market all over again. This repeat learning cycle can therefore be in somewhat of a changing market and repeat learning of how to achieve the same objectives in a different market. I also had to go from single lets to multi-lets, but this might be all change again and I might have to switch some multi-lets back to single lets. Be prepared for a lot of changes in the rental repeat learning process.

Repetition Builds Your Reputation

One positive thing that naturally comes out of repetition is that it improves your reputation. When you first start out, the others you deal with might not treat you too seriously as you have only just arrived on the scene. When you have been through the repeat processes many times, all those involved will start to treat you more seriously and with more respect.

With this can come increased opportunities whereby others can come to you with suggestions or offers of additional contacts that can help you. We have already mentioned before that estate agents are likely to start calling you to let you know of a new property that has come to market. This is much better than having to keep asking them what is new on the market. It saves a lot of time and this is simply because they are now taking you seriously because of your repeated efforts to buy more properties.

Repetition with offering work to the power team tradesmen that you use will generate loyalty and you might be able then to more easily call on them in times when you need help quickly. They can reschedule their other work to attend your job, rather than attend the job at another customer. You will recall that when you first started out, they might not have been so punctual at your jobs; that could well have been because they were putting their loyal customers' needs before yours. Now you have become that loyal customer by repeat business with them. You have to earn that status.

When you repeatedly rent out to new tenants and provide good services to them, they will recommend you to other prospective tenants. If you are taking on good tenants then good tenants normally know people of a similar nature to them, so success breeds success here with a pipeline of good tenants. Repeated advertising of property to let with your name or business name will allow you to become more established and people will start to think of you or your agency when someone wants a property to rent.

Building a reputation through repeated activities included in the BRRRR model will help you make a success of your endeavours. Repeating is the keyword in the BRRRR acronym for sure, and a major component for success. This is probably now far from what you expected the R for Repeat to mean, and the importance it actually has in the process!

Working Part-time or Full-time

Whilst you can definitely start out part-time in property investing and using the BRRRR system, there will come a point at which it will be a full-time job. Whether you do the work full-time or someone else does is going to be your choice. Of course, you could leave all this to a property management company but then you will be effectively paying for a full-time employee of theirs as well as profitability for the management company on top.

This will result in overall costs that may be a threat to the profitability of the BRRRR property business; so many landlords start a property management company of their own, as we have already discussed. You can then choose to work inside that business or have your employees work and manage it for you. That will of course very much depend on the capability of the employees and their ability to manage the many different aspects of property management I have already mentioned.

It may however also be possible to have this all managed through a separate rental agency but you will need to look carefully for one that can meet your requirements and at a budget that is appropriate for your income and expenditure levels. Add to this the caveats I have already given about handing out your property management to others, that should complete the picture and be enough for you to make a decision on which way you prefer to go.

Setting up a company does create additional responsibilities of company accounting as well as having staff to manage and an office to take care of. You will have to weigh it all up and see what you think is the best thing for you. One thing is for certain that you cannot continue to grow your portfolio and expect to manage it all yourself. We have already covered why focus on the details of the business can be counter-productive to its health in any case.

When I got to around 30 properties (including some HMOs), it did start to get too much to manage. Add to this that I was working at the time on an employed basis with a totally different business, it came to the point where I decided to set up a company and take on a full-time employee. I was still available for the business to assist in its operation, but it did allow me to even work away abroad and keep things running fairly smoothly.

The crunch point of things being too much to manage for you will come at a certain point. That point will all depend on how smooth the tenancies run and how long the average tenancy is. It will not depend solely on the number of properties as such. This, altogether, will have a bearing on how often you will need to repeat your property refurbishments. These are activities that will then need to be managed on a repeating basis.

I got to the point where I had enough refurbishments of existing properties that I had little room to take on extra purchases for continuing the BRRRR process. For me, that defined a slowing down of the BRRRR investment process and settling in of running the existing rental stock. New properties are still being purchased and refurbished, but at a much slower pace than before. If you have high ambitions to carry on *ad infinitum* then you will need to set up the company operation to support that initiative.

I think the conclusion is clear: you can start part-time but you will need to have the operation managed full-time at some point, be that by you or by others. This is not exactly the passive income you might have come to expect was waiting for you at the end. However, with a business set up to run by itself then you will get close to it, but that is the same for any business, not just a property business.

Climbing the Investing Ladder

When you start out with BRRRR investing you will probably be buying what are known as 'vanilla' buy-to-let investments, these are the simple small single let properties common to most property investors. It is wise to start at this level and start to understand the basics of property investment and property management. Depending on the location, type, and kind of finance you have with certain properties you might also be able to try short term lets, like holiday lets even though you might not be in a holiday area.

Then after a while, you might seek more ambitious projects requiring additional knowledge and skills like investing in and converting properties to HMOs. HMO management can be very demanding so you will learn a lot there too. The cash flow is much higher but so are the expenses and problems that can arise with many different households under the same roof. Add to that you need more of a focus on maintaining very high occupancy levels in order to make your HMO strategy work well.

Following on from this you might decide to branch out into property developing and selling properties for a profit. Some do deal-packaging for other investors when they know where to get the best deals from but are not interested to take any more such deals on for themselves. Property refurbishment and flipping the properties is another activity you can branch into as that will bring some capital injection into the business, which you might need at certain stages.

All these are different experiences that help you climb the property ladder. Some move on to purchasing full blocks of flats, or building properties to sell. You have many choices ahead of you, but you will still need to keep a focus on ensuring your BRRRR investments keep working away with the Repeating cycles in place to keep it healthy. Otherwise, you are better to sell up the investment portfolio and leave it behind to focus on other things higher up the property investment ladder. The experience you gained on the lower rungs of the ladder will help as a great foundation of experience and knowledge for what awaits you higher up.

Congratulations on mastering the Repeating activities!

Step Five of BRRRR(R!) completed.

If done correctly, you not only repeated the buying of further investment property, you repeatedly rented your property, and repeatedly refurbished your property, then from this you gained a good reputation as a serious property investor.

RETIRE!

The Missing Step

I have not seen the additional 'R' placed at the end of BRRRR before, to give BRRRR(R!). I am not claiming to be the first to do that, but probably that is the case. To me, the extra R is an obvious step to take to make sense of all the R's behind it. The final R is for Retire of course which is surely the objective of most people getting into property investment in the first place. Property circles abound with the promises of passive income, which has an implication of retiring from working life and doing whatever you want when you want.

Many commentaries on property investing are at least honest enough to say it is not a 'get rich quick' venture, and more a get rich slowly approach. There are however those who claim to replace their day jobs in a very short space of time through property investing. I would rather take the camp of the former and add that it takes a considerable amount of time and effort and in no way can it be considered passive income at the outset.

Retirement is about the long game and if you start early enough then it is likely you can generate your income for your retirement years from your property income. To be realistic about it I would say this could take a few decades at a minimum when there is only moderate house price growth. It is going to depend on when you invested in property in relation to the property price cycle that will have a strong bearing on how long it takes. To be on the safe side we should consider a few decades at least.

There may be ways to achieve financial independence more quickly through property investment, but that will be using alternative approaches to BRRRR. It will more likely involve a strong element of property trading, land development, property development and other such larger property projects.

However, some also look to serve existing property investors through training courses and mentorships as well as selling packaged property deals to them to generate cash more quickly. There are many examples of this in the property forums and on Facebook, as well as probably in your email inbox.

This Chapter on the last 'R' for Retirement, might not seem like it is going to be the most exciting read. However, it is written specifically to relate to someone with a property portfolio grown through BRRRR, which I can speak from experience about. I would actually go as far as saying it is probably the most important and reflective content you will have read so far. This is mainly because it should be a driver for all that you have considered and will likely add more structure to what you are doing.

Selling-up or Taking Cashflow

For most 'ordinary' BRRRR investors, they will have stayed focussed on the management of their properties, then over time, they will be at a stage where they can consider retiring from active property involvement. When it comes to this stage, they have two basic options and their property retirement income will come from one of two avenues. This can either be via the free cash flow generated from their rental income, or via the selling up of the property portfolio to a capital sum from which to live on and invest for further financial returns.

In the case of taking profits from rental income, this might be from properties that are still mortgaged or from unencumbered properties where they have paid down their mortgages over time. The latter situation will present a far less pressured environment from when they can take their income as there is nothing that can practically cause them to lose money. This is unlike where the mortgages are still in place and the interest rates could rise unexpectedly, with potentially devastating effects.

Continuing to hold the properties on an interest-only mortgage is quite possible nowadays. This will require the LTV and the property income to be in a very comfortable position for the lender to offer a mortgage to an older person, but it is entirely possible. If the investor has got to this stage, they can probably hold the properties like this and take income for the rest of their lives, no matter at what age they retired.

These kinds of good cash-flowing properties will likely always be welcome to some lenders, no matter what your age. This is especially so if there is a considerable amount of equity in the property that gives them the security for the loan. As time goes by and rents rise then properties can give positive cash flow more easily, especially if these have not been remortgaged to release equity generated from the rising market. Because of this, you don't need to plan to sell at all if you don't want to. There may also be tax advantages to this, but you would need to speak to a tax advisor about your particular circumstances

Paying down the mortgage balance is however what many investors would rather do. This means they can leave the properties in their will and leave what many investors term as a 'legacy' for future generations. There are some tax-efficient ways to do this, but that is beyond the scope of this book to go into. In any case, you should seek professional tax advice on your personal situation and optimise around that. The only thing to be sure about is that the tax adviser is very well versed in property taxes. (I find the general tax adviser is left struggling to find effective solutions to many of the recent changes to property taxation.)

We need to consider of course the money you will keep if you sell your properties. If you plan to sell, take expert tax advice first before deciding to do so. If you have interest-only mortgages then you will probably be paying off the capital element of the mortgage with property sale proceeds. In this case, you are just left with whatever increase in property value there has been due to a rising market (less, of course, any capital costs associated with purchasing, improving and selling the property). This will be profit and therefore will be subject to taxation.

With repayment mortgages, you will steadily own more and more of the property with each mortgage payment. When you sell, that part of the sale proceeds will be free of tax because you have already paid it off effectively from after-tax money, coming from either rental profits or other proceeds. If you have fully repaid your mortgage, you can retain the full original capital sum when you end up finally selling, only the increase in value element will be subject to taxation.

At the end of the term of the Repayment mortgage, there is no loan capital left to pay off. This is in contrast with the interest-only mortgage that will need to have the means to pay off the capital at the end of the mortgage term.

Building up a portfolio size of more than double what you want to keep would be one way to allow for the selling of more than half of them to pay off the debt. This is assuming you held these until prices more than doubled since first investment, allowing for the taxes payable. This would be one practical approach and this has the benefit that you are getting capital appreciation from a large property portfolio, albeit with more management responsibility.

Another approach is to convert to a repayment mortgage when the rental income increases sufficiently to absorb the increased mortgage payments and still maintain positive cash flow after all costs. It is likely to take over a decade or so to get to this position, depending on the stage of the property cycle that you are in when you buy. Of course, it can take a little less or even much longer, depending on rental market price increases. It also depends where you are in the country, as rent, as well as house prices, increase at different levels in different places.

You could take a separate savings account approach, where you would still have to either invest very well initially or else wait to be generating a sufficient free-cash-flow amount. By sufficient this would mean enough to be able to pay into a savings scheme at the required rate to build up the required capital pot to pay off the loans by a date you are planning towards.

Some of the more typical saving schemes include an endowment policy, employer's pension plan, personal pension, and an Individual's Savings Account (ISA). This is something you would need to take some advice on by consulting a qualified financial advisor.

However, this should always be compared to the value you could be generating by paying down the loan amount, which of course depends on the mortgage interest rates you are paying. It hopefully goes without saying that, if you take this approach of paying down the loans instead, you should be paying off the ones with the highest interest rates first.

The advantage of using a separate savings account is that the money is always there in case you need it to invest in something for further capital gain such as when buying and selling property. The degree of accessibility to these funds will, of course, depend on the savings scheme you have chosen. If accessibility is important to you, take this into account when choosing a savings scheme. Be aware of the Government protection limits available for savings based on each savings account and spread the savings to make sure you are covered with this protection; your bank can advise you concerning this.

The possibility of using the cash saved as a means of buying bargain property (or other assets) and then selling at a profit means it is harder for a financial advisor to compare the difference between this and simply paying off your mortgages. However, it is something that you should not fail to take into account because it offers the opportunity to make significant capital sums over timescales of less than a year.

Because you will already be in the property business, you have the skills to manage this effectively and so it becomes a real option to you and probably something you would even enjoy doing. Before jumping into this though, be sure to learn the subtle but important differences to account for in buying-to-sell; otherwise, you might end up working for nothing or even losing money. It's not the same as buy-to-let, although many of the skills are of course easily transferable.

There you have it: your BRRRR retirement options summarised, and ways to achieve each one carefully laid out before you. You don't need to take a decision on which way is best for you straight away. However, doing this sooner rather than later would be better, you can then tailor your investing strategy around that. Your property retirement objective might well affect the number of properties you are targeting buying and over what time period you are going to do this. It may also affect whether you need to carry out additional activities to meet your retirement objective. These are very fundamental matters as far as your investment strategy goes which are driven by your retirement planning.

Property as a Pension?

Having said all that I have said above, you might be surprised to hear that it makes my blood boil when I hear people talking about a property as a pension. Some have even written books asserting such, books that direct you to attend their expensive training sessions on the topic of course or offering to help buy and manage properties for you. I would like to take some time to make a distinction between what property investors define as a pension and what a true pension really is.

In property investment, there are no tax breaks that you would have with a true pension, quite the contrary. I remember having a heated 'discussion' on a well-known property forum with the author of just such a book, or rather one of his defending business partners I think it was; this was after I pointed out that it was fundamentally wrong to assert that property is a pension.

If we are to call a property portfolio a pension, then we should say the same about any business. I worry about this comparison simply because it can trick people into thinking they are building a pension in property and then they totally miss out on the benefits of having a pension vehicle in place as well. I built up both; don't just rely on one of them.

The benefits of a pension from a tax point of view are too great to be ravaged by those who seek to replace a legitimate pension vehicle with a false equivalent. Not to mention the insult when this is solely to sell people books, training courses, and mentorships about running a property business. This is an outrage as far as I am concerned.

However, as you can see from the previous discussion, I do appreciate that property profits can form an income that can be used in your retirement years. Only that would be true of any good business that can be set up to run itself and generate a surplus of cash after covering all costs.

If you are going into property full-time, like the advocators of using a property as a pension might want to take you into, you will in fact have more of a challenge with setting up a true pension. This is because when you are employed, the pension is generally set up for you with the employer's scheme and you don't have to do anything. You will be benefiting automatically from the tax breaks it brings; this is both in terms of breaks on income tax as well as breaks on taxation of pension scheme annual profits.

However, you should take advice on setting up a true pension if you don't have one already. You will need to explain your situation and your future objectives and try to get a pension solution totally separate from the property income that you are working on generating. You can then benefit from the great tax breaks there currently are with pensions, as well as the flexibilities recently introduced in accessing private pension money after the age of 55.

A proper pension discussion would be a book in its own right, and maybe a worthy one specifically for property investors who can actually get a lot of synergy from pensions investments, if they make the right choices. That is a matter for discussion another day maybe, although most of the books on Small Self-Administered Scheme (SSAS) pensions will give some good information on this matter. These books are mostly written by property investors and therefore have a naturally property investing angle about them.

The point here is that you should not fall for the trap of just solely relying on your property business as future pension income and miss out on the benefits that a pension brings for saving, to truly fund your retirement years.

What is Retirement, Anyway?
If you research the word *retirement*, you will find many definitions of it. If it is taken to its fullest extreme it is a total withdrawal from working life. You therefore maybe want to ask yourself concerning when you would really want to retire. There is the middle ground of course of semi-retirement, and that is a good option to many as they wind down from their working lives before going into full retirement. If you do retire in the fullest sense, what will you do with your life?

Many people find meaning in what they do and out of that they get a sense of wellbeing as they contribute to society with what they do. It would be much better for this kind of person to carry on contributing by doing some work of some kind than simply withdrawing from doing anything that could be considered as work. Maybe a more modern definition of retirement is now emerging that is along the lines of being able to do what you want to do, when you want to do it.

If we take that definition then you can see that normal daily work life would not allow you to do that. Whereas if you don't have to work a regular pattern, you can consider that you comply with that to some extent, while still doing meaningful tasks. You could still therefore be working and retired at the same time, if you take the definition given above. Again, the classification often given to this is *semi-retired*; although to me this is a little bit more retired than that due to the additional freedom you can have.

Continuing to be active in business in 'retirement' might well resonate with many property investors who have an entrepreneurial spirit in their lives. This spirit is then released into action when they come into the world of property and they break out of solely working for a living. This can be quite a liberating feeling and one that they might not want to give up on in their lives so easily.

On that subject, I recall having a forum debate with someone who said they were looking to stop property as they were approaching retirement. In the end, we concluded that in fact, property investment was their life and not a job as such. Despite their age, they found they enjoyed working in property investment so much that they did not want to stop and wanted to carry on into retirement.

This was a great revelation for this person because they had been programmed to think they had to stop doing what they liked doing when they reached a certain age. Certainly, you might find there are many aspects to property investment that you can get very involved with. For some people that is something they take to very well and enjoy doing. There may also be some of the positives of property investment that even makes any of the hassles that you can get from it very worthwhile for some people.

The warning I would give here however is that for whatever reason, property investors should be aware that it can easily take over their lives. There are also many property investor communities that makes your involvement in property somewhat of a competition and that could become another reason for keeping on going. There will always be someone you can look up to and wish you were in their position, which might become a reason to keep on going and going. This is not what I was talking about when I mentioned retirement can still be defined differently from what is considered the norm.

Be careful that if you get into this situation and want to keep on going in property, do this in a totally considered way and make sure you are happy that when you get to the end of your life, you would not have wanted to do anything else instead. After all, many people get into property investment with the promises they hear of financial freedom and all that this can bring to a person, to enable them to do what they want to do. It is likely that working in property all their lives was not what they originally had in mind at the time.

Setting Your Retirement Date

Whichever way you might want to define *retirement*, you need to set a date against being in that state by a certain age. This will create focus on what you are doing today with your BRRRR strategy, to make sure it will serve you in your objectives. We have already discussed how retirement planning will affect your investment strategy and the date sharpens that up and starts to put timescales on things. Without a timescale and just an objective alone, you really don't have a plan, you just have an idea of what you want to do.

Even if you decide to change that date later because of some changes to your life, that does not matter, you simply need a date to be able to set a plan and see how that might affect your BRRRR endeavours. There is no right or wrong age for this of course and it depends a lot on how old you are now and when you are starting out in property, at least as far as planning your BRRRR objectives it does. I would also say that for some, our current age can affect what is possible in a certain timescale.

This is because you probably won't have the energy and drive you have in your younger years. To this end, it is a distinct advantage if you start as soon as possible and not delay unnecessarily. The younger you are the more likely you will be able to sustain the focus and energy that is required in managing all the aspects of BRRRR, especially if you start out doing this while you are still in full-time employment. That will probably be the case for the majority of people, as it was for me.

At least there is an advantage in the BRRRR process that as you get further into it, you should be in a position to generate the income to pay for the help in managing the business. Most of your personal energy is needed at the start to get things moving and get the rental income generation activated, as well as maintained of course.

This is likely to be the loneliest part of your journey with BRRRR and the time about which you will need to draw most on your inner reserves and determination to succeed. You will be working in your business as well as on your business. Lessons will be coming at you thick and fast as the learning curve will be a sharp one, despite all you might do to prepare yourself beforehand.

Will You Ever Really Retire?

If we take the strict definition of retirement which we have already discussed, and if you take the approach of keeping your properties rather than selling up, there is a likelihood that you will never fully retire. You will be able to minimise your involvement but there will always be something that will command your input at some stage as at least an interruption to your day.

It all gets back to what you really want from the final R in BRRRR(R!). We have discussed the options already in terms of keeping the properties for cash flow or selling up. Each has different merits as you will have seen. The decision might not be an easy one, especially if you sell up and then see the property prices increase over just a few more years from when you sold. That is basically a fact of investment and choosing the right time to leave a market can be a bit of a gamble, as none of us knows the future.

The notion of retirement has become a little blurred in recent years due to the change in the ways people earn a living. The old way of working for a company for many years and then taking a work-related pension is now reducing drastically, especially as pensions are changing with less security in this area being offered by many of the larger employers.

Another way to look at this is to ask yourself whether the things you want to do in life, outside of property investment, can be done with or without you continuing to work. Maybe this is the most important thing and not whether you technically retire or not. As an example, many people want to see the world, and in normal times this will need both money and time. You will therefore need to at least have a business that can run without your daily involvement if you want to keep the property business.

If you retire early and need to have the money to fund such activities for an unforeseen amount of time then you will need something that can continue to deliver the funds you need. That is more likely to be a business of some kind, which would push the pendulum more to keep the properties rather than disposing of them and taking a lump sum of cash. The other option of course is to invest that lump sum of cash to produce income, however, to get decent returns nowadays there will be some element of investment risk you might not want to take at such a late stage in life.

Financial Freedom & Retirement

Financial Freedom is a term that is often given out in property circles, it would do you well to understand how this differs from retirement. For some people, it might seem to be exactly the same thing. We often hear that financial freedom is when you make the same money from passive income as you were making from the job you were in when that was the sole income you had. This is usually in the context of passive income from property of course, although there are other sectors that claim the same definition, such as in online marketing for example.

The difference might therefore be very minimal to some, in fact when many people take a pension, they actually get much less than what they were earning. That drop in income is however supposed to be tolerable due to the fact that living expenses will have fallen, chiefly because most people will have paid off the mortgage on their own home by retirement age. Here we are defining financial freedom as being the same passive amount, or more, than our earned income level; hence more than a pension as such.

The rub on this is the fact that many of the claimed passive earnings giving financial freedom are in fact not very passive at all. That includes property investing, especially using the BRRRR model that we are focussing on here. It is a matter of really switching your professions rather than becoming truly financially free. I define truly financially free as being in a position where you don't have to do anything to pay the bills you incur during daily life, and the source meeting those obligations will be there for the rest of your life.

I often hear people claiming they retired at say 45, yet they are very active in a property business they have created. Given the definitions of retirement we have already discussed, this is not retirement and it is not financial freedom. It is simply that they have created another job or business that they are active in. We have already mentioned that this might well be what such an entrepreneurial person really wants and has found new life having broken away from a job they may well not have liked. To me however, this is not retirement and not even financial freedom.

What they are doing however could be setting them up on the path of achieving both and so this is not to criticise what they are doing, only to challenge the terminology that is often used by them. I hope this discussion helps clarify some of the terminologies you hear and gives you chance to have a double-take on what they are saying and reveal the real situation, at least so you can properly understand their possibly erroneous terminology (I won't say misleading).

For you, it should now be clear what you are aiming for, which might even be financial freedom before retirement, whether that be full retirement or semi-retirement. Not only what you are aiming for but by when. In this way you will at least be in charge of your plan for the future, whether circumstances allow that to work out may be an entirely different thing, but you can only plan for that which you are in control of. Let fate take care of any differences, but at least you will have done your part in steering, although maybe not fully controlling, your own destiny.

Other Retirement Pensions Options

In addition to the capital or revenue to fund your retirement from your BRRRR, and any other, property ventures, you should have other irons in the fire in case problems arise. One recent problem for many who were planning to use BRRRR to fund their retirement was the introduction of the Section 24 tax we have already discussed. That will have either reduced or eliminated any cash flow that some people might have been expecting to live on. That was just on the whim of a past chancellor but it is now something that will have a major effect on the plans of many property investors for years.

We simply don't know what is around the corner. The way the Government treats landlords with rising taxation and increasing legislation means you should not be surprised about getting any more such major surprises if that makes sense? The issue here is that it does not seem to matter which political party is in power, no political party seems to have the landlord's interests at heart.

Landlords are relatively few in number and tenants are large in number; this means, for vote-winning, it makes sense for all political parties to appeal to the tenants rather than landlords. Therefore, I don't ever see there being a landlord-friendly political party, unless they socially need landlords more desperately to provide the housing that they can't.

You have been forewarned. The action that should come out of this is to check that you have other forms of retirement income in place and not just relying on the one source from your property investment endeavours. That could see you left high and dry if some changes come along with anything similar to the devastating effects of Section 24. We might not hear much about those effects as the media won't be interested to publicise it, that is because they are also biased on the unfairness towards tenants rather than the plight of landlords.

We have already discussed the benefits of having a proper pension in place, which will benefit you from good tax breaks. Pensions are always under review by the Government and so this could be an area for another attack in future, especially now as they seek to recover from the financial disaster of the Coronavirus they have had to fund. It is therefore best that you review your true pension situation as soon as you can.

At least with pensions if the Government makes any adverse changes, it is likely to negatively affect their popularity, which they won't want to happen. This means that pensions are much more likely to escape a taxation attack than a landlord's income is, for the reasons already explained.

Pension advice is best to come from a qualified pensions adviser, the only advice I can give you is to make sure they are not a restricted adviser who will be either limited to a range of products or a limited number of providers. You need to get truly independent advice from an independent pensions adviser. You should therefore specifically ask whether they are a restricted or independent adviser. Don't be persuaded by any follow-up chat if they try to explain away how they have the best products, even though they are restricted. You really should take fully independent advice.

If you are fully versed in pensions then you will not have too much to learn from what I am about to say. I would expect that most readers will not be very well conversant in this area. I know that most people are not. Even very educated people with high-paying jobs seem to bury their heads in the sand when it comes to the subject of pensions, I have seen that first hand.

For many people, it might even be beneficial to spend some time researching this area of pensions option so that you are not easily taken advantage of by any adviser, whether independent or not. I find that even independent advisers may have an agenda to recommend certain providers or products that might not be in your best interest, even though they should view things only from your point of view. Although they may be registered with the Financial Conduct Authority, there are some outcomes I have seen that would leave you wondering. (Speaking from personal and painful pensions 'advice' experience there.)

The pension options you have open to you will likely depend on your attitude to risk as well as your age. A pensions adviser can take you through the options available once they have taken a look at your financial situation and assessed your attitude to risk. You should also let them know about your property portfolio or your intentions, as well as any other business-related activity you are considering, for them to give you their very best advice.

I will now give you a rough breakdown of your pensions options for you to be aware of. I can let you know about most from personal experience as I have done the rounds here.

Defined Benefit (DB) Pensions

The company *defined benefit* scheme is often seen as the best company pension available. This is called *defined* because you are guaranteed a certain outcome of income from a certain age, based on the fact that you continue to make regular pension contributions. These are what the final salary schemes were based on, which are now being reduced in number and phased out as they are costing companies too much to finance.

That is not to say these schemes give you your final salary as a pension of course, but that your pension will be based on a fraction of your final salary. This fraction will depend on the number of years you have been contributing to the scheme, but will stop at a maximum of 2/3rds. Some companies have variations on the final salary scheme where the amount you get might be based on a percentage of your average salary for the last five years of employment for example. This would stop someone from planning to take the highest position they can, only to retire soon afterwards and take the final salary figure benefits.

In other cases, a more realistic approach that has drastically reduced the pension value has been to award a pension for a defined benefit scheme as an average of their salary during their period of employment with a company. Again, this would be a fraction of this based on the number of years of employment and up to the same maximum of 2/3rds of the average figure calculated.

I was in the unfortunate position to have employment where the pension was changed from true final salary to average salary. The only benefit that I had was that it was frozen as final salary at the point of when they made the change and then adjusted going forwards as an average salary scheme. Then came the master blow when they stopped even the average salary scheme and put us on a *defined contribution* scheme, which we will discuss later.

The impact of all of this was to effectively reduce my expected pension income by less than half of what I would have expected to get from the original final salary scheme. Hence my foray into the many different pension schemes available that I can now give you the benefit of hearing about, in case it can be of help to you in any way.

We have now briefly covered the main feature of a *defined benefit* pension and it is important to assess the value this offers you if you are lucky enough to have one. You need to assess what you are giving up here if you are planning on leaving your employment to follow your BRRRR property endeavours full time. You will need to take specialist advice on this to calculate the potential cost impact to you of doing so. Your *defined benefit* pension could be a very valuable asset to have.

After the company *defined benefit* scheme was finally closed, I was automatically enrolled into a *defined contribution* scheme. This was to replace the *defined benefit* scheme as my new company pension scheme. That is when I started doing the calculations and decided on initiating the other pension changes that I can inform you about to consider too. After discussing the DB pensions CETV option, I will explain what difference the *defined contribution* scheme brought to me and why I moved my money out of it.

DB Pensions CETV Option

We will now discuss a potentially very liberating option you have with DB schemes. It should be noted however that there is an exception with what we are about to discuss with anyone in public service who will have a public service pension scheme. These include civil servants, armed forces, health service workers, teachers, judiciary, police, firefighters and local government workers as well as any public body schemes. With these schemes, there is a defined benefit pension arrangement that is paid by the Government. In these cases, you only have the option to take the pension when it is due to be paid in your retirement years.

In the case of private company defined benefit schemes, you should have the option of taking a *cash equivalent transfer.* That means you can take a lump sum as a final settlement from the company so that you then forsake any rights to a pension payment from them. The amount that you can take will depend on the scheme administrators who set the rules, but typically this could be in the range of 20 – 25 times the amount of annual income they are projecting you will take at retirement, not adjusted for inflation. This amount that you will be offered upon request is called the *cash equivalent transfer value* (CETV).

This can amount to a considerable sum yet is seen as fair and equitable to pay this by the company pension trustees, as it reduces the pension scheme liabilities later. In that way, it can work for both parties, as long as you can take this money and make it work harder for you to produce a higher annual income. Such a transfer is not to be taken lightly and any value over £30,000 will legally need the involvement of a qualified Financial Adviser.

It will be the job of this adviser to assess the situation and either recommend that it is likely to be the best thing for you to do or not. If they can recommend this then the transfer can be authorised. The financial adviser will be paid a fee for this in some form or another, and you need to discuss that with them and get competitive quotes for such work if you want to go down this route. That payment will likely be in the form of a small percentage of the amount transferred, or from ongoing pension charges from a private pension scheme they might recommend you transfer the money to.

Be aware of any redemption penalties if you take the latter-mentioned transfer payment option, as the penalties can be significant if you decide the scheme recommended is not working well for you. I got bitten by this and ended up paying around three times as much as I would have done if I had agreed on a percentage fee at transfer. That was because I realised after the transfer that it was not going to be suitable for me.

Another reason to move from the defined benefit scheme, which you may well want to consider if you have one, is that the cash transferred becomes part of your estate in your own new private pension scheme. With defined benefit schemes you lose the income when you die, any surviving spouse may well just get half of the income and when they die it ceases to be given to your family.

When you make a transfer out of a defined benefit scheme (often simply known as DB schemes for short), that money is yours but locked away under normal pension rules, only to be released according to prevailing pension tax laws. At least it is part of your wealth now, and not relying on how long you or your spouse lives to see the benefit of it in your estate.

Defined Contribution (DC) Pensions

The *defined contribution* (DC) scheme is when pension contributions made on a monthly basis are put into a scheme that then invests the money for returns. Normally this is put into the stock market which is supposed to bring reasonable returns over the long term, despite its ups and downs over the shorter term. The reason it is called defined contribution is because all that can be defined, or let's say guaranteed, is what you put in and not what you get out as a pension. What you get out will be based on how well the investments did over time, in addition to what you and the company put into the scheme.

This is as opposed to the defined benefit scheme, where you know what you will get out based on the amount of time you have been contributing and the amount of time you have been in the scheme. In this kind of scheme, you will get annual statements showing you what your pension will be based on at a certain retirement age, and assuming you stay in the company's employment until that date. With the *defined contribution* scheme, you will get an annual statement showing you the amount you and the company have contributed and what the current value of the scheme is based on the investments made.

DC schemes are also what private pension schemes consist of. You can either have a DC scheme associated with your employer as a company pension, or have one where you are paying into it independently of any employer arrangements as a private pension. Where you have a good contributory DC scheme with your employer, you can mix the two and have your own as well if that means you can have more freedom in what you can invest in.

All you have to do for this arrangement is transfer funds from your company DC scheme to your private pension DC scheme, say on an annual basis or as frequently as is allowed by the employer's scheme. You just need to leave a small amount in the employer scheme when you do this to keep it open for further contributions.

Not All Private Pensions Are Equal
Having taken advice and carried out a cash equivalent transfer to a private pension, I was now fully in charge of my own pension for the first time. When you have gained this control over your pension, you can transfer to another private scheme if you wish. In my case, it was my judgement at the time that the private pension I had moved to was going to be performing so badly that I had no option. I looked at other investment products in the same company to see if anything could be done to give me the financial returns I would be happy with, together with the security of investment that I was looking for.

It just turned out that it was not going to meet my pension objectives at reasonable costs. Therefore, that is another thing to assess if you do move the money from either a company DB or DC scheme, be careful where you move the money to. Especially if you are moving it on the basis of a free transfer from a DB scheme but subject to redemption penalties for any early transfer out of that scheme. That was the situation that I was in, but I decided to move anyway and take the hit.

The next step I took was to move the private pension to another private pension organisation that would allow me to set up a Self Invested Personal Pension (a SIPP) at a reasonable cost. This organisation also had lower annual fees, which are taken as a percentage of your pension pot each year. This is another aspect of private pension schemes that you need to be aware of, as even something below two percent can have a major effect on the size of your pension pot over the years.

The more expensive schemes are the ones that tend to offer higher returns because they say they are 'managed schemes'. That is exactly the kind of scheme I had transferred out of when I moved to a different private pension. The claim of being managed was not that great, it was just a matter of helping me choose a portfolio of paper investments in stocks and shares. There was not going to be any further advice on a regular basis it seemed, even though there were times when it was clear the market was going to go down significantly.

Fortunately, I could now have a say in where the money went and whether it was in any stocks and shares or even invested in nothing at all during a market downturn. I therefore started doing the management by requesting to pull the money out of the market when all seems to be going South. It was clear to me that there was no real value in the managed service for the amount that was being charged. I researched the market for non-advisory pension schemes and found one that would allow me to make the very same investments but at a much lower cost to the pension pot.

For me, that move was a good move, but you might find some managed services have reasonable fees which you feel more comfortable about if you don't want to be responsible for the details of your investments. I have heard from some people with such managed schemes that are very happy with that arrangement. You will have to decide what you would prefer, but of course, managed pension schemes come at a premium price.

Self Invested Personal Pensions

We now get to a stage of discussion where we partially enter back into the world of property, but this time directly through financing this with pension money. In this case, the rent income goes straight into your pension tax-free. However, for these kinds of pension schemes, you can only hold commercial property inside them, and nothing that has any element of residential nature about it, such as a shop with flats above for example. It has to be purely commercial property.

A pension that can do this is a form of private pension called a Self-Invested Personal Pension (a SIPP). Not only can it do that but it can make all the normal paper investments in the stock markets that a standard private pension can do. There are other asset classes that you can invest in as well but that depends on the company operating the SIPP. For property investors, the main thing will be that you can hold commercial property in a SIPP.

Property held in a SIPP can have absolutely no living accommodation included in it in any way whatsoever. I have seen no end of people on internet forums repeatedly asking this question as though they are willing for someone to say it is allowed. Not even mixed-use properties can be included even though they have a commercial aspect to them. It must be totally commercial, 100%.

You can also borrow money using a SIPP to 50% of the value of your total SIPP pension pot. This will also give you the chance to apply some of your skills with BRRRR inside your pension if you buy commercial property which you can refurbish and remodel. In fact, you can have the advantage with commercial property that its value can significantly increase based on the tenant and tenancy attached to it. One thing to be aware of here is that some SIPP providers will require that you only buy a property that is already let out or will be let at the time of purchasing into the SIPP.

This might not be as major a matter as you might think. By way of an example on how to deal with this, when I bought an otherwise empty property in my newly formed SIPP I became the property manager, and a company of mine became the tenant, who then sublet to the lettings company I had set up to manage my BRRRR rental properties. Other parts of the building were then let to other companies needing more office space than the lettings company needed.

You might therefore need to get a little creative about it but you can see how you can make things work. Is this now making pensions seem interesting maybe? I have not gone down the route of using BRRRR principles with pensions investments in commercial property. That is only because I 'discovered' it when I was late on with my property endeavours and approaching the final step in the retirement pension planning process. If I had my time again then this would be something very worthwhile looking at. If you are at a different stage, you might well get the interest in this as an alternative angle to BRRRR.

The advantage to you will be that you will be able to use the same power team tradesmen that you use for your residential BRRRR activities, and many of the skills are easily transferred into commercial property. There is some very different terminology to get used to, and in some cases how the same-named terms mean different things, such as *yield* for example. But it won't take long before you become both commercial and residential language 'bilingual'.

Even if you don't intend to go too heavy into commercial property, it can at least offer you an option to buy a commercial property you may need for business operations, then pay the rent directly into your pension (rather than pay someone else the rent money). If you are looking to grow your business and need office premises this then becomes another possibility. One thing which will not be possible to get away with however, is not paying the rent simply because your pension owns it. The pension provider will be very keen that you follow up on any unpaid rent, even if this means following things up with yourself!

Small Self Administered Scheme (SSAS) Pensions

The type of pension scheme that is going to align most closely with a property investors activity is a Small Self Administered Scheme (a SSAS). With this kind of pension, there will be a way to actually use some of the money in the pension to help with your property development work outside of your pension. This does not mean that you can buy residential property, as just like with the SIPP, you have to only buy commercial property to hold inside a SSAS too. Rather, this means if you set up a company that is trading, with say doing property refurbishments or developments, you can give a loan to that company from your pension and then pay it back to the pension later at an interest rate you have control over.

It could also be used to purchase commercial properties that you are going to convert to residential property, however, it must then be sold to another company at the point at which it is classed as residential property. This is because there is a very strict condition on any pensions that they cannot hold residential property, but if you are clever about it there are ways you can use it to fund your residential property ventures.

Because you will be loaning money from your pension fund you will then be paying your interest on loaned money into something that will be benefiting you in the longer term. This might already start to sound much better than using bridging loans, where the loan companies benefit from you.

As with SIPPs, there are other asset classes that you can also invest in with a SSAS, and these can allow the widest possible range of investments in any kind of pension. So much so that it is more like running a small business than having a simple pension scheme. You will need good record keeping as a SSAS's operational detail needs recording and getting approval with HMRC, who will also monitor that it is being used according to the strict investment rules. To this end, you will probably need the services or what are known as a professional trustee. For an administration fee they will help keep your books in order and your investments in line with the legal requirements.

One thing that is important to know about such professional SSAS administrators is that not all scheme administrators are the same. Each administrator will have decided on what elements of a SSAS they are willing to administer. That means you might not have access to all the possible investment options that you are legally allowed to have. This restrictive list of investments is called a *mandate*.

What you are best to do is to look for a scheme administrator that does not have such a mandate and can therefore get you the best possible flexibility from your investment approach. You therefore want to ask such a prospective scheme administrator about their mandate and hope they say they don't have one!

There is no better and more flexible pension scheme than a SSAS for a property investor. I moved my SIPP to a SSAS recently. In my time investing with BRRRR I was fully using the basic approach with mortgaging and remortgaging, but if I had owned a SSAS pension at the time, I would have been able to access more cash to fuel the investment process.

However, that would only have been possible if I had also had a trading business. Why is that? Here is another thing you need to know about a SSAS pension: it cannot be set up using a shell company or Special Purpose Vehicle (SPV), you need to have an active company ideally one that has employees and paying tax via P.A.Y.E.

This is another thing to weave into your BRRRR planning if you are looking to take advantage of such a kind of pension for all the benefits that it can bring you. It can most easily be done as I did it if you don't have any other business that could fall into this category.

I used my property management company to be the so-called sponsoring company for the SSAS pension set-up. This most naturally fits what you will be doing with your BRRRR investing as you get more mature and you decide to do the management under your control, rather than use other agents. This in itself could be a reason to consider this approach, at least it would be another factor when thinking about whether to use agents or set up your own.

As well as buying commercial property inside my SSAS, I now invest in Property Development Loans (PDLs) using an FCA registered peer-to-peer lending platform. You might also find this appropriate when you do reach the stage of retirement or semi-retirement and you don't have any development programmes of your own going on. Instead, you can put your property knowledge into continued action by helping others who need property development money, by selecting the best deals that give you a good return for a minimum of risk.

Investing in PDLs is another topic in its own right, and I could not even start to go into some of the key aspects here. But suffice for you to know at this stage that it exists and is an option for you with the right pension vehicle in place. If you were even to sell your BRRRR portfolio and bank the capital made, you could invest in PDLs outside of a pension. In this case the loan interest paid to you will be subject to usual taxations that exist outside of a pension vehicle.

Tax Residency Freedoms

One of the things you will have the option of considering when you reach this stage of retirement or semi-retirement could be the selection of a different place in the world to live. Technology is such now that you can even keep in touch with your property operations back in the UK while you are living aboard and without excessive expense.

Due to recent changes in taxation that has been targeting landlords, many larger landlords have looked seriously into their options and changing tax residency is one option. Different countries have different requirements for you to be tax resident with them, some make it attractive and others not so attractive. There might also be requirements like having to invest in a property there or at least have a long-term rental agreement on one. You will need to research these at the time but some come with low- or no-income-tax for foreign-derived income.

Don't think that this will help you too much with your property taxes as any property owned by you in the UK will come under UK tax. However, if you operate inside a company, you will have the chance of taking earned income and dividends at a much lower rate than you would in the UK. This can vary significantly depending on your personal situation and your business structures, so we can only talk very generally here.

There are some countries that require you to be physically resident in the country to gain residency for tax purposes and others that don't. However, what is for sure is that you need to be out of the UK for minimum periods of time. The amount of time you need to be absent will depend on your situation in the UK and these are called *ties* to the UK. This will be up to a maximum average of 90 days per year in the UK over a continuous period of 6 years to gain UK non-residency status, with a maximum stay of 180 days in any one qualifying year.

A tax adviser can update you on the latest situation and let you know what you need to achieve for non-UK residency; although they won't be able to help too much with the foreign residency aspect and you will need local help for that. You therefore need to know what you need to do on both sides of the equation. There are some combinations that give you freedom to live anywhere, except the UK of course. An example of this would be to take non-habitual residency (NHR) in Portugal by simply buying or renting a property at a certain qualifying amount and live in another country. You would then come under the NHR taxation for Portugal.

In my case, I had reasons to consider Costa Rica and there are benefits in taxation there for no tax on foreign-derived income. This means you can take earnings made from outside of Costa Rica into the country free of tax, as long as you earn this as an individual and not a Costa Rican registered corporation. As stated before, you will still have UK property tax obligations to fulfil, but you could charge for consultancy services to your UK operations for example and take tax-free income that way. This will be possible even during the 6 years period, as you have earned that while living in another country.

You might immediately think of more local countries such as Spain for retirement or semi-retirement, but look carefully at the tax implications as you might be jumping out of the frying pan into the fire if you are not careful. This is a complex area but it could offer you tax advantages in retirement when you don't need to be physically based in the UK to support your property and other business operations. This makes it worthy of further study.

Planning Your Legacy and Inheritance

Having a legacy to pass on to future generations is something that I hear a lot about in property circles. It seems that this is one of the drivers for many people for some reason. I cannot share in that sentiment so I can't expand much further on that, only to say you will need to plan for this. Some of the steps I have taken at the end of my main BRRRR activities are now preparing for this, even if it is a biproduct of other things I am seeking. I will therefore be able to share with you some ideas on this matter, in case that is of interest to you.

In terms of the inheritance of your estate, this is something that will happen whether you plan it or not, but as to who gets this and how tax efficiently, will only be decided by any purposeful action you take. If you don't plan anything and depending on your family or lack of immediate family, it might even end up with the Government if you don't say otherwise. I can't think of a worse place for it to end up personally. I am sure you will want to avoid that too.

These matters are perhaps far from your mind if you are only just starting out on your BRRRR ventures. Maybe it is a topic for later, but the sooner you sort these matters out the better and smoother things will be for others when the inevitable happens. I can't go into all the details here but just give you enough to think about and have separate discussions with appropriately qualified tax advisers and solicitors.

Dealing with protecting your legacy and minimising inheritance taxation liabilities give rise to the same protective actions. Assuming you have your Will written to assign where your assets will go when you die, you should then consider the tax efficiency of this transfer. In some cases, this could put whoever you transfer them to under quite some pressure for inheritance tax. This can lead to forced quick sales of some of the properties to pay the demanded inheritance tax. The urgency required will very likely lead to a lowering of the value of the asset base.

You should therefore consider how you hold the properties and maybe include them in a trust for example. One example of such would be a Limited Liability Partnership (LLP), this will allow for membership or association of others who you have included in your will. When you die the LLP does not die and therefore can take the pressure off property sale immediacy for meeting inheritance tax obligations.

This is just an example and as ever with these matters, you need to get advice on your specific circumstances. The purpose of this final short section was just to get you to think about these matters and put them on the agenda as part of your holistic business planning exercise. Your inheritors will be happy that you paid attention to such detail and your legacy may then get off to a good start. It won't happen by accident.

Congratulations on Retiring early!

Final Step Six of BRRRR(R!) completed.

If done correctly, you not only retired early but set up your retirement vehicles to benefit from your experience gained as a property investor using BRRRR, which was the means that led to the end. Enjoy the rest of your life, whether that be still with an element of property investment or not, as is your choosing.

Conclusion

We have looked at each of the various topics of BRRRR(R!) in detail, including many matters associated with the practical side of property investment in the UK. Of course, some of this will apply to property investing in any part of the world; although I have dealt with matters peculiar to the UK in some detail, which is my experience, and in particular in England. The information has been organised by each general topic area, which is reflected in each chapter title.

I hope this has given you some good insights into what to expect. If you are already into property investment, maybe there were a few 'light bulb' moments as you read the lessons. As I have been investing for more than 16 years now, I will have experienced most of what you can expect will come at you at some stage of your investment career. I therefore hope there was something of value to you in the various chapters. If you did not find anything of particular value, then you can safely consider you have mastered BRRRR and are ready to put the final 'R' at the end (at least in terms of planning for it).

As you continue in property investment, keep up to date with the changes in this area by involvement with others and by reading or otherwise educating yourself as you develop. However, the one area I spotted that was not well covered was that of financing buy-to-let properties, which was the reason I wrote the book *All About Buy-to-Let Mortgages* a few years ago. The information in that book is still current, I will update it with later editions when anything significant changes.

I recommend you go through that book, in whatever format you choose (paperback, kindle, or audible), and then select your financing and your mortgage broker carefully in line with the information given in the book. Financing is the lifeblood of property investment and in particular in BRRRR and it can also have a great impact on your bottom-line profits. It is very worthwhile making this effort to study that book if you are serious about going deeper into UK property investing.

As you can see, I am generally trying to deliver information into this property space where there is a lack of details on such topics. I am happy to share my experience and my learning over the years so that you can do even better than I have. At my stage of investing, I feel mature enough to be able to write and pass this information on for your benefit.

I have additional information available from my website and additional support materials you can benefit from, both paid and free materials. By registering for either of these, we can also keep in touch and I can inform you when I have anything you may benefit from in the future.

For access to this further information and to keep in touch please visit my website www.buy-to-let-mortgages.org.uk and sign up as either a FREE or paid member, getting access to additional valuable information.

I wish you all the luck and strength you need to be successful in UK property investment. You have my utmost respect as you continue in this challenging field of business. You deserve all the benefits you can get. In fact, I will now switch my attention to writing the sequel book that focusses on the benefits of property investing, now this book is complete. As already stated, that will be a sequel book to my second book *UK Property Investment: The Toxic Truth!* and will have the very apt title of *UK Property Investment: The Antidote!*

I hope to see you soon in another book, either in the book called *All About Buy-to-Let Mortgages*, where I go into details on using mortgages in the financing of No Money Left In deals; or in the book called *UK Property Investment: The Toxic Truth!* where I give you a 'heads up' on what possible challenges await you (you will do well to be prepared!).

Finally, some people have approached me, requesting me to help them directly with their property investing endeavours. This is to give them support in either starting or developing their property investing businesses. I have therefore now decided to make myself available for those who may want or need that level of support.

My main objective will be to help such people avoid the many traps that often catch other people out, and ends up costing them a lot of money in mistakes. In addition, I will look at ways of maximising their opportunities, as they go about their property investing activities. This is all based on my 16 years of property investing experience, as well as knowledge gained from my attendance on the many different property training courses, where I have picked up many additional profitable tips.

If you are interested in such ongoing property investing support, please simply send me an email to express your interest. To do this, just write 'Investing Support Request' in the email subject line and send your email to contact@peterjhow.com. I will then get back to you to gather some specific details from you, in order to see if I am the right person to offer you the support you need.

Best Wishes.

Peter J How

P.S. I want to ask a favour from you in giving this book a Review on Amazon, or any other platform from which you may have made the purchase. If you did not buy it from an internet platform, please leave me a review on Amazon in any case. This will encourage me to write more materials and hopefully from that, I can assist you further in your property investing endeavours.

P.P.S. If this book has enlightened you, or struck a chord with you at all, you may want to consider getting the same book but in audiobook format. This is what I have heard quite a few readers do, so they can easily recap on the topics you have read about. It enables better memory retention of the useful points presented in the book. And don´t forget my further resources and materials, both free and paid versions, available at my main website www.buy-to-let-mortgages.org.uk

Printed in Great Britain
by Amazon